THE AUSTRALIAN
Women's Weekly
sauces
salsas & dressings

acp
books

contents

BÉCHAMEL, BEURRE BLANC, ESPAGNOLE, VELOUTE AND MAYONNAISE ARE THE FIVE BASIC AND ADAPTABLE "MOTHER" SAUCES WITH MORE THAN 200 YEARS OF FRENCH HISTORY BEHIND THEM.

tip If the béchamel is too thick, whisk in up to ¼ cup warm milk until the sauce reaches desired consistency.
to reheat Place in small saucepan over very low heat, stirring until just heated through.
goes well with pasta dishes like pastichio or lasagne; grilled fish fillets.
what went wrong If sauce is lumpy, push through fine sieve into small bowl.
the traditional French béchamel is based on a roux, a cooked butter and flour mixture used as a thickening agent for many sauces. Béchamel can be eaten as is, or used as the basis for other sauces, four of which follow on page 7.

classics

béchamel

preparation time 5 minutes **cooking time** 15 minutes **makes** 1 cup

30g butter
2 tablespoons plain flour
1¼ cups (310ml) hot milk
pinch nutmeg

1 Melt butter in medium saucepan, add flour; cook, stirring, until mixture bubbles and thickens. Gradually add milk, stirring, until mixture boils and thickens. Stir nutmeg into sauce.
per tablespoon 3.1g total fat (2.1g saturated fat); 176kJ (42 cal); 2.6g carbohydrate; 1.1g protein; 0.1g fibre

parsley

preparation time 5 minutes **makes** 1 cup

1 cup (250ml) warm béchamel sauce (page 4)
¼ cup finely chopped fresh flat-leaf parsley

1 Combine ingredients in small bowl.
tip Don't stir the parsley into the béchamel until you're just ready to serve it.
goes well with corned beef; poached white fish fillets.
per tablespoon 3.1g total fat (2g saturated fat); 176kJ (42 cal); 2.6g carbohydrate; 1.1g protein; 0.1g fibre

mornay

preparation time 5 minutes
cooking time 5 minutes **makes** 2 cups

1 cup (250ml) béchamel sauce (page 4)
¼ cup (60ml) cream
1 egg yolk
1 cup (120g) coarsely grated
   emmentaler cheese

1 Bring béchamel to a boil in medium saucepan; add cream and egg yolk, whisk 1 minute.
2 Remove sauce from heat; add cheese, stir until cheese melts.
tip Substitute gruyère or cheddar for emmentaler.
goes well with lasagne; cauliflower or broccoli au gratin; oysters.
per tablespoon 4.4g total fat (2.8g saturated fat); 222kJ (53 cal); 1.4g carbohydrate; 2.2g protein; 0.0g fibre

soubise

preparation time 5 minutes
cooking time 20 minutes **makes** 2 cups

40g butter
1 large white onion (200g), sliced thinly
1 cup (250ml) béchamel sauce (page 4)
¾ cup (180ml) cream
pinch nutmeg

1 Melt butter in medium saucepan; cook onion, stirring, over low heat, until softened.
2 Add béchamel and cream; simmer, uncovered, stirring constantly, about 5 minutes or until soubise thickens. Stir in nutmeg.
tip If finished soubise is too thick, whisk in up to ¼ cup warm milk.
goes well with poached eggs; white fish fillets.
per tablespoon 5.7g total fat (3.7g saturated fat); 238kJ (57 cal); 1.4g carbohydrate; 0.4g protein; 0.1g fibre

seafood

preparation time 10 minutes
cooking time 15 minutes **makes** 2 cups

1 cup (250ml) dry white wine
1 cup (250ml) béchamel sauce (page 4)
¾ cup (180ml) cream
250g marinara mix, drained
2 tablespoons finely chopped fresh dill
1 tablespoon lemon juice

1 Bring wine to a boil in medium frying pan then reduce heat. Simmer, uncovered, until reduced by half.
2 Add béchamel, cream and marinara mix to pan; bring to a boil then reduce heat. Simmer, uncovered, about 5 minutes or until seafood is cooked through. Stir in dill and juice.
goes well with grilled white fish fillets; pasta; grilled beef fillets.
per tablespoon 5g total fat (3.2g saturated fat); 293kJ (70 cal); 2.1g carbohydrate; 2.7g protein; 0.1g fibre

beurre blanc

preparation time 10 minutes **cooking time** 10 minutes **makes** 1 cup

¼ cup (60ml) dry white wine
1 tablespoon lemon juice
¼ cup (60ml) cream
125g cold butter, chopped

1 Combine wine and juice in small saucepan; bring to a boil. Boil, without stirring, until reduced by two-thirds. Add cream; return to a boil then reduce heat. Whisk in cold butter, piece by piece, whisking between additions, until sauce is smooth and thickened slightly.

per tablespoon 10.4g total fat (6.8g saturated fat); 406kJ (97 cal); 0.3g carbohydrate; 0.2g protein, 0.0g fibre

variations

toasted sesame and chilli beurre blanc After butter has been added, stir in 2 teaspoons toasted sesame seeds and 1 finely chopped fresh small red thai chilli.
roast garlic and lemon beurre blanc Roast eight garlic cloves in moderately hot oven (200°C/180°C fan-forced) about 15 minutes or until garlic softens. When cool enough to handle, peel; chop garlic finely. Stir garlic and 2 teaspoons finely grated lemon rind into beurre blanc after butter has been added.

makes enough for six 200g servings of salmon fillets.
tip Do not allow sauce to boil when adding butter.
also goes well with steamed vegetables; grilled chicken breast fillets; steamed or poached fish fillets.
what went wrong Do not add butter too quickly, otherwise mixture will separate.
translated as "white butter", this classic French emulsified sauce is composed of a white wine and lemon juice reduction into which chunks of cold butter are whisked until the sauce is thick and smooth.

espagnole

preparation time 15 minutes **cooking time** 1 hour 10 minutes **makes** 1 cup

2 teaspoons olive oil
900g beef sirloin
2 medium carrots (240g), chopped coarsely
4 shallots (100g), quartered
2 trimmed celery stalks (200g), chopped coarsely
2 teaspoons plain flour
1 tablespoon tomato paste
2 cups (500ml) beef stock
1 cup (250ml) water

1 Preheat oven to moderately hot (200°C/180°C fan-forced).
2 Heat oil in large flameproof casserole dish; cook beef, uncovered, over high heat until browned. Place dish in oven; roast, uncovered, about 45 minutes or until beef is cooked as desired.
3 Remove beef from dish; cover to keep warm. Place dish with pan juices over high heat, add carrot, shallot and celery; cook, uncovered, stirring occasionally, about 10 minutes or until vegetables are well-browned. Add flour; cook, stirring, about 4 minutes or until mixture is dark brown. Add paste, stock and the water; bring to a boil. Boil, uncovered, about 10 minutes or until sauce thickens.
4 Strain sauce, discard vegetables. Slice beef; serve with espagnole.
per tablespoon 7.7g total fat (3.2g saturated fat); 615kJ (147 cal); 2.3g carbohydrate; 16.6g protein; 1g fibre

makes enough for four 220g servings of beef sirloin.
tip If using purchased stock, make sure sauce does not overly reduce or it will become bitter and salty.
also goes well with roast venison; roast kangaroo.
a basic brown sauce, based on a roux, espagnole is traditionally made from meat stock, a selection of browned vegetables, flour, herbs and sometimes tomato paste. While it is eaten on its own, it usually has various different ingredients added and takes a new name. Espagnole sauce suits game and red meat best.

chicken velouté

preparation time 5 minutes **cooking time** 30 minutes **makes** 1½ cups

2¼ cups (560ml) chicken stock
40g butter
2 tablespoons plain flour

1 Place stock in small saucepan; bring to a boil then remove from heat.
2 Melt butter in medium saucepan, add flour; cook, stirring, about 2 minutes or until mixture bubbles and thickens. Stir in hot stock gradually; bring to a boil. Cook, stirring, until sauce boils and thickens.
3 Reduce heat; simmer, uncovered, about 20 minutes or until reduced by half. Strain sauce into small bowl.
per tablespoon 2g total fat (1.3g saturated fat); 100kJ (24 cal);
1.1g carbohydrate; 0.5g protein; 0.1g fibre

makes enough for four 200g servings of chicken breast fillets.
also goes well with poached chicken; as the sauce for a chicken or mushroom pie filling.
what went wrong If sauce is lumpy, you may have added the stock too fast or not incorporated it thoroughly between additions. Push sauce through fine sieve into medium bowl, discarding any remaining solids.
velouté, which translates from the French as "the texture of velvet", is similar to a béchamel except for the fact that a light stock is added to the roux instead of milk. If you're serving this sauce with fish, replace the chicken stock with fish stock; for a vegetarian version, use vegetable stock. Velouté and its variations (see page 12) should be served as soon as they are made.

mushroom velouté

preparation time 10 minutes
cooking time 15 minutes **makes** 2½ cups

20g butter
1 small brown onion (80g), chopped finely
150g button mushrooms, sliced thinly
¼ cup (60ml) dry white wine
1½ cups (375ml) chicken velouté (page 11)
¼ cup (60ml) cream

1 Melt butter in medium saucepan; cook onion, stirring, until softened. Add mushrooms; cook, stirring, about 5 minutes or until softened.
2 Add wine to pan; cook, stirring, until almost all liquid evaporates. Add velouté; bring to a boil.
3 Add cream; reduce heat, stir until sauce is heated through.

goes well with pasta; as a chicken and bacon pie filling; over sweetbreads.

per tablespoon 2.6g total fat (1.7g saturated fat); 130kJ (31 cal); 0.9g carbohydrate; 0.6g protein; 0.2g fibre

spinach and nutmeg velouté

preparation time 15 minutes
cooking time 15 minutes **makes** 2 cups

20g butter
1 clove garlic, crushed
1½ cups (375ml) chicken velouté (page 11)
⅓ cup (80ml) cream
pinch nutmeg
½ teaspoon ground black pepper
200g baby spinach, shredded finely

1 Melt butter in medium saucepan, add garlic; cook, stirring, 1 minute.
2 Add velouté; stir over low heat for 5 minutes.
3 Add cream, nutmeg and pepper; bring to a boil then reduce heat. Add spinach; simmer, stirring, 5 minutes.

goes well with roasted artichokes; grilled zucchini; stirred through pasta.

per tablespoon 3.6g total fat (2.4g saturated fat); 163kJ (39 cal); 1g carbohydrate; 0.7g protein; 0.3g fibre

saffron and lemon velouté

preparation time 10 minutes
cooking time 15 minutes **makes** 2 cups

1½ cups (375ml) chicken velouté (page 11)
2 egg yolks
1 tablespoon lemon juice
¼ teaspoon saffron threads
¼ cup (60ml) cream

1 Place velouté in small saucepan; bring to a boil, remove from heat. Combine egg yolks, juice, saffron and cream in small bowl; gradually whisk into hot velouté.
2 Stir, over low heat, until heated through.

goes well with seafood; steamed green beans, broccoli or asparagus.

per tablespoon 3g total fat (1.8g saturated fat); 138kJ (33 cal); 1g carbohydrate; 0.7g protein; 0.1g fibre

caramelised apple and mustard velouté

preparation time 10 minutes
cooking time 20 minutes **makes** 2 cups

2 large apples (400g), unpeeled
20g butter
1 tablespoon brown sugar
1½ cups (375ml) chicken velouté (page 11)
1 tablespoon dijon mustard

1 Remove core from apples; cut into 16 wedges.
2 Melt butter in medium frying pan; cook apple, uncovered, until browned lightly both sides.
3 Add sugar and velouté to pan. Stir in mustard. Cook, stirring, until sauce is heated through.

goes well with baked ham; roast game; baked brie or camembert.

per tablespoon 2.2g total fat (1.4g saturated fat); 138kJ (33 cal); 2.9g carbohydrate; 0.5g protein; 0.3g fibre

mayonnaise

preparation time 15 minutes **makes** 1 cup

2 egg yolks
½ teaspoon salt
¾ teaspoon mustard powder
⅔ cup (160ml) extra light olive oil
⅓ cup (80ml) olive oil
1 tablespoon white vinegar

1 Combine egg yolks, salt and mustard in medium bowl. Gradually add oils, in thin, steady stream, whisking constantly until mixture thickens. Stir vinegar into mayonnaise.

per tablespoon 19.1g total fat (2.8g saturated fat); 715kJ (171 cal); 0.0g carbohydrate; 0.5g protein; 0.0g fibre

tip For best results, whisk ingredients in glass bowl with balloon whisk.
storage Mayonnaise will keep under refrigeration for up to three days in a screw-top jar.
cheat's way Blend or process egg yolks, salt and mustard until smooth. With motor operating, gradually add oils in thin, steady stream. Add vinegar; blend or process until mayonnaise thickens.
what went wrong Oil must be added slowly to prevent mixture separating. Should mixture separate, whisk in 1 tablespoon hot water.
homemade mayonnaise, an emulsion made from egg yolks and oil, is usually more flavoursome than its store-bought cousin. It can be used as a basis of a number of different sauces (see page 17), or used as a sauce for meats and vegetables, as a sandwich filling, salad dressing or dipping sauce.

CLASSICS

remoulade

preparation time 20 minutes **makes** 1 cup

1 cup (250ml) mayonnaise (page 14)
1 tablespoon finely chopped cornichons
1 tablespoon drained, rinsed baby capers,
  chopped finely
1 tablespoon dijon mustard
1 drained anchovy fillet, chopped finely
2 teaspoons finely chopped fresh flat-leaf parsley
2 teaspoons finely chopped fresh tarragon

1 Combine ingredients in small bowl.
storage Remoulade will keep under refrigeration for
up to three days in a screw-top jar.
goes well with pan-fried breaded fish fillets; grilled
chicken breasts; steamed or roasted vegetables.
*per tablespoon 9.6g total fat (1.4g saturated fat);
364kJ (87 cal); 0.2g carbohydrate; 0.3g protein;
0.0g fibre*

tartare

preparation time 20 minutes **makes** 1 cup

1 cup (250ml) mayonnaise (page 14)
2 tablespoons finely chopped cornichons
1 tablespoon drained, rinsed baby capers,
  chopped finely
1 tablespoon finely chopped fresh
  flat-leaf parsley
2 teaspoons finely chopped fresh dill
2 teaspoons lemon juice

1 Combine ingredients in small bowl.
storage Tartare sauce will keep under refrigeration
for up to three days in a screw-top jar.
goes well with grilled chicken breasts; smoked
or fried fish.
*per tablespoon 9.5g total fat (1.4g saturated fat);
364kJ (87 cal); 0.3g carbohydrate; 0.3g protein;
0.0g fibre*

thousand-island dressing

preparation time 20 minutes **makes** 2 cups

1 cup (250ml) mayonnaise (page 14)
¼ cup (60ml) tomato sauce
½ small white onion (40g), grated finely
8 pimiento-stuffed green olives, chopped finely
1 small red capsicum (150g), chopped finely

1 Combine ingredients in small bowl.
storage Thousand-island dressing will keep under
refrigeration for up to three days in a screw-top jar.
goes well with grilled fish; cold or hot seafood platters;
as a sandwich spread.
*per tablespoon 9.6g total fat (1.4g saturated fat);
385kJ (92 cal); 1.3g carbohydrate; 0.4g protein;
0.2g fibre*

aïoli

preparation time 20 minutes **makes** 1 cup

4 cloves garlic, quartered
1 teaspoon sea salt
2 teaspoons lemon juice
1 cup (250ml) mayonnaise (page 14)

1 Using mortar and pestle, crush garlic and salt
to a smooth paste.
2 Combine garlic mixture and remaining ingredients
in small bowl.
storage Aïoli will keep under refrigeration for up to
three days in a screw-top jar.
goes well with grilled fish fillets; crudités;
fried or boiled potatoes.
*per tablespoon 19.1g total fat (2.8g saturated fat);
719kJ (172 cal); 0.2g carbohydrate; 0.6g protein;
0.2g fibre*

hollandaise

preparation time 5 minutes   **cooking time** 15 minutes   **makes** 1 cup

2 tablespoons water
2 tablespoons white vinegar
¼ teaspoon cracked black pepper
2 egg yolks
200g unsalted butter, melted

1   Combine the water, vinegar and pepper in small saucepan; bring to a boil then reduce heat. Simmer, uncovered, until liquid reduces to 1 tablespoon. Strain through fine sieve into medium heatproof bowl; cool 10 minutes.

2   Whisk egg yolks into vinegar mixture until combined. Set bowl over medium saucepan of simmering water; do not allow water to touch base of bowl. Whisk mixture over heat until thickened.

3   Remove bowl from heat; gradually add melted butter in thin, steady stream, whisking constantly until sauce has thickened.

per tablespoon 14.5g total fat (9.2g saturated fat); 548kJ (131 cal); 0.1g carbohydrate; 0.5g protein; 0.0g fibre

makes enough for six servings of eggs benedict, a breakfast or brunch specialty consisting of toasted english muffin halves topped with ham, poached egg and hollandaise sauce.
tip If hollandaise is too thick, or separates, whisk in up to 2 tablespoons of hot water until mixture is smooth and creamy.
also goes well with steamed asparagus; grilled fish.
cheat's way Blend or process egg yolks and hot vinegar mixture until combined. With motor operating, add melted butter in thin, steady stream until hollandaise is of desired consistency.

tomato

preparation time 10 minutes   **cooking time** 40 minutes (plus cooling time)
makes 3½ cups

1 tablespoon olive oil
1 large brown onion (200g), chopped coarsely
2 tablespoons brown sugar
3 x 400g cans diced tomatoes
¼ teaspoon ground allspice
½ teaspoon celery salt
2 tablespoons tomato paste
⅓ cup (80ml) white vinegar

1   Heat oil in large saucepan; cook onion, stirring, until soft. Add sugar, undrained tomatoes, allspice and celery salt; bring to a boil then reduce heat. Simmer, uncovered, stirring occasionally, about 30 minutes or until mixture thickens. Stir in paste and vinegar; cook, uncovered, 5 minutes.

2   Blend or process sauce until smooth; push through fine sieve into medium bowl. Discard solids. Serve sauce cold.

per tablespoon 0.5g total fat (0.1g saturated fat); 63kJ (15 cal); 1.9g carbohydrate; 0.3g protein, 0.5g fibre

tips If tomatoes are in season, coarsely chop 1.8kg and substitute for the canned variety. Sauce can be kept, covered, in the refrigerator for up to one month; also suitable to freeze.
goes well with grilled white fish fillets; sirloin steak; pork sausages.
also called ketchup, catsup and even catch-up, this thick, spicy sauce is a traditional American accompaniment to french fries, scrambled eggs, hamburgers and hot dogs. The vinegar gives this sauce its tang, while sugar, salt and spices contribute to the overall flavour.

béarnaise

preparation time 20 minutes **cooking time** 5 minutes **makes** 1 cup

2 tablespoons white vinegar
2 tablespoons water
1 shallot (25g), chopped finely
2 teaspoons coarsely chopped fresh tarragon
½ teaspoon black peppercorns
3 egg yolks
200g unsalted butter, melted
1 tablespoon finely chopped fresh tarragon

1 Combine vinegar, the water, shallot, coarsely chopped tarragon and peppercorns in small saucepan; bring to a boil then reduce heat. Simmer, uncovered, about 2 minutes or until liquid reduces by half. Strain over medium heatproof bowl; discard solids. Cool 10 minutes.

2 Whisk egg yolks into vinegar mixture until combined. Set bowl over medium saucepan of simmering water; do not allow water to touch base of bowl. Whisk mixture over heat until thickened. Remove bowl from heat; gradually whisk in melted butter in thin, steady stream until béarnaise thickens slightly. Stir finely chopped tarragon into sauce.

per tablespoon 15.1g total fat (9.5g saturated fat); 577kJ (138 cal); 0.2g carbohydrate; 0.8g protein; 0.0g fibre

makes enough for four 220g servings of grilled beef sirloin steak.

cheat's way Blend or process egg yolks and hot vinegar mixture; with motor operating, add melted butter in thin steady stream until thick.

also goes well with grilled fish fillets; pan-fried chicken breast fillets; steamed or boiled vegetables.

what went wrong If sauce separates, whisk in about 1 tablespoon boiling water until mixture is smooth.

If sauce is too thick, whisk in up to 2 tablespoons of hot water until the desired consistency is reached.

béarnaise is very similar to hollandaise with the flavour bonus of tarragon, black pepper and shallots.

italian dressing

preparation time 5 minutes **makes** 1 cup

⅔ cup (160ml) olive oil
⅓ cup (80ml) lemon juice
1 clove garlic, crushed
2 teaspoons finely chopped fresh oregano
2 teaspoons finely chopped fresh basil
2 teaspoons caster sugar

1 Place ingredients in screw-top jar; shake well.

per tablespoon 12.2g total fat (1.7g saturated fat); 468kJ (112 cal);
0.9g carbohydrate; 0.1g protein; 0.1g fibre

makes enough to dress 400g salad leaves.
also goes well with steamed or boiled vegetables; grilled lamb.

french dressing

preparation time 5 minutes **makes** 1 cup

⅓ cup (80ml) white wine vinegar
2 teaspoons dijon mustard
½ teaspoon sugar
⅔ cup (160ml) olive oil

1 Combine vinegar, mustard and sugar in small bowl.
2 Gradually add oil in thin, steady stream, whisking constantly until mixture thickens.

per tablespoon 12.2g total fat (1.7g saturated fat); 456kJ (109 cal);
0.2g carbohydrate; 0.0g protein; 0.0g fibre

makes enough to dress 400g salad leaves.
also goes well with any type of salad or salad greens.
cheat's way Place ingredients into screw-top jar; shake well.
french dressing is a simple oil-and-vinegar combination. You can add a tablespoon of freshly chopped fresh herbs of your choice to this recipe, if desired.

makes enough to dress a large Caesar salad (cos lettuce, croutons and parmesan flakes) to serve six people.

also goes well with roast chicken; grilled prawns; crab salad; salad greens.

cheat's way Place ingredients in blender or processor, add egg, blend briefly; gradually add oil in thin, steady stream; blend until mixture thickens slightly.

what went wrong If oil is added too quickly mixture will separate.

most historians believe that the Caesar salad takes its name from restaurateur Caesar Cardini, who invented it in Mexico in 1924 on the Fourth of July holiday weekend. Business was brisk so Cardini, when food started to run low, tossed together a salad for his guests from what was left in the kitchen.

caesar dressing

preparation time 10 minutes **cooking time** 5 minutes **makes** 1½ cups

1 egg
2 cloves garlic, crushed
½ teaspoon dijon mustard
2 drained anchovy fillets, chopped finely
1 cup (250ml) olive oil
2 tablespoons lemon juice

1 Bring water to a boil in small saucepan; using slotted spoon, carefully lower whole egg into water. Cover pan tightly, remove from heat; after 1 minute remove egg from water using slotted spoon. When cool enough to handle, break egg into large bowl; whisk in garlic, mustard and anchovy.

2 Gradually add oil in thin, steady stream; whisking until mixture thickens slightly. Stir in juice.

per tablespoon 13g total fat (1.9g saturated fat); 493kJ (118 cal); 0.1g carbohydrate; 0.5g protein; 0.1g fibre

CLASSICS

cumberland

preparation time 5 minutes **cooking time** 30 minutes (plus cooling time)
makes 1 cup

1 shallot (25g), sliced thinly
½ cup (125ml) red wine vinegar
½ cup (125ml) port
½ teaspoon finely grated lemon rind
½ teaspoon finely grated orange rind
¼ cup (60g) red currant jelly
1 cup (250ml) beef stock

1 Place shallot and vinegar in small saucepan; bring to a boil then reduce heat. Simmer, uncovered, until mixture reduces by half.

2 Add remaining ingredients; bring to a boil then reduce heat. Simmer, uncovered, about 20 minutes or until mixture is reduced by half. Strain into small jug. Cool sauce to room temperature.

per tablespoon 0.1g total fat (0.0g saturated fat); 159kJ (38 cal); 6.1g carbohydrate; 0.7g protein; 0.0g fibre

makes enough for six 200g servings of smoked chicken.
cumberland sauce, an English sauce served cold with poultry, game or ham, should be fairly clear and of a thin consistency.
storage Cumberland sauce will keep under refrigeration for up to one week in a screw-top jar.

sabayon

preparation time 5 minutes **cooking time** 5 minutes **makes** 2 cups

3 egg yolks
¼ cup (55g) caster sugar
¼ cup (60ml) dry white wine

1 Combine ingredients in medium bowl set over medium saucepan of simmering water; do not allow water to touch base of bowl. Whisk vigorously and continually about 5 minutes or until sauce is thick and creamy.

per tablespoon 0.6g total fat (0.2g saturated fat); 71kJ (17 cal); 2.3g carbohydrate; 0.3g protein; 0.0g fibre

variations

lime sabayon Add 1 teaspoon finely grated lime rind and 2 teaspoons lime juice to sabayon ingredients before whisking over simmering water.

coffee sabayon Dissolve 2 teaspoons instant coffee granules with ¼ cup water in small jug; use instead of wine with ingredients before whisking over simmering water.

makes enough for six servings of grilled peaches or nectarines.
also goes well with poached pears; fresh mango slices.
what went wrong A flat sabayon is the result of underwhisking. You must whisk vigorously to incorporate as much air as possible. Cooking the mixture too quickly will make the sabayon too thick; prevent this by keeping the water in the saucepan at a low simmer.
sabayon, a French variation of the Italian dessert zabaglione, is a light, frothy custard sauce often used as a filling for pies and tarts.

SEAFOOD
ALWAYS TASTES
BEST IF IT'S
COOKED SIMPLY.
SERVING IT WITH
A SPOONFUL OF
SAUCE MAKES
IT WONDERFUL.

sauces for seafood

makes enough for two uncooked 750g crabs, enough to serve four. **Singapore chilli crab** is this island nation's unofficial national dish and, like Singapore itself, is an amalgam of the best of its Malaysian, Indian and Chinese past.

singapore chilli crab

preparation time 10 minutes   **cooking time** 20 minutes   **makes** 2 cups

1 tablespoon peanut oil
1 small brown onion (80g), chopped finely
½ teaspoon cayenne pepper
400g can crushed tomatoes
1 tablespoon soy sauce
2 tablespoons brown sugar
2 cloves garlic, crushed
3cm piece fresh ginger (15g), grated
1 fresh small red thai chilli, sliced thinly
1 teaspoon cornflour
½ cup (125ml) water

1   Heat oil in wok; stir-fry onion until softened. Add pepper, undrained tomatoes, sauce, sugar, garlic, ginger and chilli; bring to a boil then reduce heat. (Add prepared crabs to wok at this point). Simmer 15 minutes.
2   Add blended cornflour and the water to wok; stir until tomato mixture boils and thickens.
per tablespoon 0.8g total fat (1.4g saturated fat); 67kJ (16 cal); 1.9g carbohydrate; 0.3g protein; 0.3g fibre

cantonese vegetable

preparation time 20 minutes **cooking time** 5 minutes **makes** 1 cup

2 tablespoons soy sauce
2 tablespoons mirin
1 tablespoon honey
⅓ cup (80ml) orange juice
¼ cup (60ml) water
1 teaspoon five-spice powder
1 star anise
1 clove garlic, crushed
2cm piece fresh ginger (10g), cut into matchsticks
1 small carrot (70g), cut into matchsticks
3 green onions, sliced thinly
65g drained bamboo shoots, cut into matchsticks

1 Combine sauce, mirin, honey, juice, the water, five spice, star anise and garlic in small saucepan; bring to a boil then reduce heat. Add ginger, carrot, onion and bamboo shoots; simmer, uncovered, about 5 minutes or until vegetables are tender and sauce thickens slightly.
per tablespoon 0.0g total fat (0.0g saturated fat); 71kJ (17 cal);
3.1g carbohydrate; 0.4g protein; 0.4g fibre

makes enough for four 200g servings of poached or steamed snapper.
also goes well with grilled white fish fillets; poached chicken breasts.

sweet and sour

preparation time 10 minutes **cooking time** 10 minutes **makes** 2 cups

565g can lychees in light syrup
1 teaspoon cornflour
⅓ cup (80ml) water
2 tablespoons white sugar
2 tablespoons white wine vinegar
2 tablespoons tomato sauce
2 tablespoons soy sauce
1 teaspoon peanut oil
1 small red capsicum (150g), chopped coarsely

1 Drain lychees over small bowl, reserving ¼ cup of the syrup. Halve lychees.
2 Blend cornflour with the water in medium jug; stir in sugar, vinegar, sauces and reserved syrup.
3 Heat oil in large frying pan; cook capsicum and lychee, stirring, until capsicum softens. Add cornflour mixture; stir until sauce boils and thickens slightly.
per tablespoon 0.2g total fat (0.0g saturated fat); 92kJ (22 cal);
4.8g carbohydrate; 0.3g protein, 0.2g fibre

makes enough for eight 200g servings of grilled fish fillets.
tips Fresh lychees can be substituted for canned ones if you like. You can use pineapple and pineapple juice instead of lychees for a different flavour.
also goes well with fried tofu; grilled chicken breasts; steamed greens.

leek and saffron

preparation time 8 minutes **cooking time** 10 minutes **makes** 1½ cups

makes enough for six 180g servings of ocean trout fillets.
also goes well with grilled chicken breasts; pan-fried pork cutlets; grilled white fish fillets.

1 tablespoon olive oil
1 small leek (200g), halved lengthways, sliced thinly
2 cloves garlic, crushed
1 teaspoon plain flour
¼ cup (60ml) dry white wine
300ml cream
pinch saffron
1 tablespoon finely chopped fresh flat-leaf parsley

1 Heat oil in medium frying pan; cook leek and garlic, stirring, about 5 minutes or until leek softens. Add flour; cook, stirring, 1 minute or until mixture bubbles and thickens. Add wine; cook, stirring, until sauce boils and reduces by half.
2 Add cream and saffron; bring to a boil then reduce heat. Simmer, uncovered, about 5 minutes or until sauce thickens slightly. Stir in parsley off the heat.
per tablespoon 8.3g total fat (4.9g saturated fat); 339kJ (81 cal); 0.9g carbohydrate; 0.5g protein; 0.3g fibre

white wine

preparation time 5 minutes **cooking time** 20 minutes **makes** 1 cup

makes enough for six 180g servings of pan-fried ocean perch fillets.
also goes well with grilled or barbecued prawns; grilled lobster.

20g butter
2 shallots (50g), chopped finely
1 teaspoon mustard powder
¾ cup (180ml) dry white wine
¾ cup (180ml) fish stock
300ml cream

1 Melt butter in medium frying pan; cook shallot and mustard powder, stirring, about 3 minutes or until shallot softens. Add wine; cook, uncovered, until wine reduces by two-thirds. Add stock; bring to a boil. Boil, uncovered, about 7 minutes or until reduced by half.
2 Add cream to pan; bring to a boil then reduce heat. Simmer, uncovered, about 15 minutes or until sauce thickens slightly.
per tablespoon 12.4g total fat (8.1g saturated fat); 531kJ (127 cal); 1g carbohydrate; 0.9g protein, 0.0g fibre
variations
sun-dried tomato Add 1 tablespoon sun-dried tomato pesto to sauce after sauce has thickened.
horseradish and dill Add 1 tablespoon horseradish and 1 tablespoon finely chopped dill to sauce after sauce has thickened.
lime and green onion Add 2 thinly sliced green onions, 1 teaspoon finely grated lime rind and 1 tablespoon lime juice to sauce after sauce has thickened.

warm dill and lemon

preparation time 5 minutes **cooking time** 5 minutes **makes** ½ cup

⅓ cup (80ml) olive oil
1 teaspoon caster sugar
2 teaspoons finely grated lemon rind
¼ cup lemon juice
2 tablespoons finely chopped fresh dill

1 Heat oil in small saucepan until just warm. Remove from heat.
2 Stir in remaining ingredients.
per tablespoon 12.2g total fat (1.7g saturated fat); 472kJ (113 cal);
1g carbohydrate; 0.1g protein; 0.1g fibre

makes enough for
four 220g servings
of salmon fillets.
tip Add a tablespoon of
drained, rinsed baby
capers to the oil,
if desired.
also goes well with
grilled squid; pan-fried
chicken or duck breasts.

rouille

preparation time 10 minutes **cooking time** 10 minutes **makes** 1 cup

1 medium red capsicum (200g)
1 cup (70g) stale breadcrumbs
¼ cup (60ml) water
1 fresh small red thai chilli, chopped finely
1 clove garlic, quartered
1 tablespoon lemon juice
½ teaspoon cayenne pepper
¼ cup (60ml) olive oil

1 Quarter capsicum; discard seeds and membrane. Roast under preheated grill
or in very hot oven, skin-side up, until skin blisters and blackens. Cover capsicum
pieces in plastic or paper 5 minutes; peel away skin then chop coarsely.
2 Combine breadcrumbs and the water in small bowl; stand 2 minutes.
3 Blend or process capsicum and breadcrumbs with chilli, garlic, juice and
pepper until smooth.
4 With motor operating, gradually add oil in thin, steady stream; process until
rouille thickens.
per tablespoon 4.8g total fat (0.7g saturated fat); 280kJ (67 cal);
4.6g carbohydrate; 1.1g protein; 0.5g fibre

makes enough for six
275g servings of pan-
fried snapper fillets.
tip Rouille can be made
a day ahead. Cover;
refrigerate overnight.
also goes well with
cioppino (fish stew);
grilled white fish fillets;
pan-fried chicken breasts.
what went wrong If
rouille separates, add
about 1 tablespoon of
boiling water to mixture
and whisk until smooth.
French for "rust", rouille
is so-called because of
its deep-red colour. A
capsicum- and chilli-
flavoured sauce, it is
often used to enhance
seafood stews such
as bouillabaisse.

olive, anchovy and tomato

preparation time 15 minutes **cooking time** 15 minutes **makes** 1½ cups

makes enough for six 200g servings of grilled fish steaks.
also goes well with pan-fried sirloin steaks; barbecued pork cutlets; grilled pork fillets.

2 teaspoons olive oil
1 medium brown onion (150g), chopped finely
2 cloves garlic, crushed
3 drained anchovy fillets, chopped finely
¼ cup (60ml) dry red wine
425g can diced tomatoes
½ cup (125ml) water
1 tablespoon white sugar
2 tablespoons coarsely chopped black olives
1 tablespoon drained, rinsed baby capers
3 drained anchovy fillets, chopped coarsely
¼ cup finely chopped fresh flat-leaf parsley

1 Heat oil in large saucepan; cook onion, garlic and finely chopped anchovy, stirring, about 5 minutes or until onion softens. Add wine; cook, uncovered, about 2 minutes or until mixture reduces by half.
2 Add undrained tomatoes, the water and sugar to pan; bring to a boil then reduce heat. Simmer, uncovered, about 10 minutes or until sauce thickens slightly.
3 Stir in olives, capers, coarsely chopped anchovy and parsley.
per tablespoon 0.7g total fat (0.1g saturated fat); 92kJ (22 cal); 2.3g carbohydrate; 0.7g protein; 0.5g fibre

chermoulla

preparation time 15 minutes **makes** 1 cup

makes enough for four 200g servings of grilled fish fillets.
also goes well with grilled quail; fried white fish fillets; barbecued squid or octopus.
chermoulla is a Moroccan blend of herbs and spices traditionally used for preserving or seasoning fish or meat. We used our chermoulla blend here as a quick sauce for fish or seafood, but you can also use it as a baste or marinade.

½ cup (125ml) olive oil
⅓ cup (80ml) lemon juice
6 shallots (150g), sliced thinly
4 cloves garlic, crushed
1 teaspoon ground cumin
1 fresh long red chilli, sliced thinly
¼ cup finely chopped fresh coriander
¼ cup finely chopped fresh mint
¼ cup finely chopped fresh flat-leaf parsley

1 Combine ingredients in small bowl; mix well.
per tablespoon 9.6g total fat (1.3g saturated fat); 376kJ (90 cal); 0.7g carbohydrate; 0.3g protein, 0.4g fibre

POULTRY IS SO ADAPTABLE THAT IT TASTES EQUALLY GOOD WITH SAUCES MADE FROM INGREDIENTS AS DIVERSE AS CHILLI AND CREAM.

sauces for poultry

coconut and kaffir lime leaf

preparation time 10 minutes **cooking time** 10 minutes **makes** 1 cup

makes enough for four 200g servings of pan-fried chicken breast on the bone.
also goes well with steamed yellow rice; grilled prawns.
kaffir lime leaves, also known as bai magrood, are sold fresh, dried or frozen; they look like two glossy dark green leaves joined end to end forming a round hourglass shape.

1 teaspoon peanut oil
1 clove garlic, crushed
2cm piece fresh ginger (10g), grated
1 teaspoon finely chopped coriander root and stem mixture
1 tablespoon finely chopped fresh lemon grass
4 fresh kaffir lime leaves, sliced thinly
140ml can coconut milk
½ cup (125ml) chicken stock
2 teaspoons fish sauce
1 tablespoon lime juice
1 teaspoon caster sugar
2 tablespoons finely chopped fresh coriander

1 Heat oil in medium frying pan; cook garlic, ginger, coriander root and stem mixture, lemon grass and half of the kaffir lime, stirring, until fragrant.
2 Add coconut milk, stock, sauce, juice and sugar; bring to a boil then reduce heat. Simmer, uncovered, about 3 minutes or until sauce thickens slightly. Strain into small jug; stir in remaining lime leaf and finely chopped coriander.
per serving 2.9g total fat (2.2g saturated fat); 134kJ (32 cal);
1g carbohydrate; 0.5g protein; 0.3g fibre

SAUCES FOR POULTRY

red nam jim

preparation time 15 minutes **makes** 1 cup

3 fresh long red chillies, chopped coarsely
3 fresh small red chillies, chopped coarsely
1 shallot (25g), chopped coarsely
2 cloves garlic, crushed
2cm piece fresh ginger (10g), chopped coarsely
⅓ cup (80ml) lime juice
2 tablespoons fish sauce
1 tablespoon grated palm sugar
¼ cup (35g) finely chopped unsalted roasted peanuts

1 Blend or process chillies, shallot, garlic, ginger, juice, sauce
and sugar until smooth. Stir in nuts.
per tablespoon 1.4g total fat (1.2g saturated fat); 109kJ (26 cal);
1.8g carbohydrate; 1.1g protein; 0.5g fibre

makes enough for four
200g servings of grilled
chicken thigh cutlets.
tip Use either fewer
chillies or milder fresh
green chillies to reduce
the heat of this sauce.
also goes well with
grilled fish; thai beef
salad; stir-fried rice
noodles; as a dip.
nam jim is a generic
term for a thai dipping
sauce; most versions
include fish sauce and
chillies, but the remaining
ingredients are up to the
cook's discretion.

piri piri

preparation time 15 minutes **makes** 1½ cups

2 cloves garlic, chopped finely
6 fresh long red chillies, chopped finely
2 tablespoons dijon mustard
⅔ cup (160ml) lemon juice
½ cup (125ml) olive oil

1 Combine ingredients in small bowl; mix well.
per tablespoon 6.4g total fat (0.9g saturated fat); 251kJ (60 cal);
0.4g carbohydrate; 0.2g protein; 0.1g fibre

makes enough for four
servings of barbecued
butterflied spatchcocks.
tip Baste spatchcocks
with half of the sauce
as they cook; remove
spatchcocks from pan.
Add remainder of sauce
to same pan. Bring to
a boil; simmer, stirring,
2 minutes.
also goes well with
grilled fish fillets; grilled
vegetables; stirred into
a cup of sour cream and
eaten as a dip.
a Portuguese hot
sauce, piri piri is used
for marinating meats or
poultry, brushing over
grilling foods, or as an
ingredient in cooking.

deglazing

makes enough for four 200g servings of pan-fried chicken breast.
also goes well with roast turkey; pan-fried lamb backstraps.

deglazing This is the initial step in making a sauce that incorporates the browned bits sticking to the bottom of a pan in which meat has been cooked. A small amount of liquid is added to any remaining meat juices in the pan, then over heat, the pan is scraped to loosen the browned caramelised bits. After the mixture is combined, flour is often stirred in to make a roux-like basis for the sauce; other times, cream or butter will be added to create a richer, more velvety sauce.

makes enough for four 200g servings of pan-fried chicken breast.
tip If sauce is too tart, add a little more honey.
also goes well with whole roast turkey, duck or chicken.

diable

preparation time 10 minutes cooking time 35 minutes
serves 4 makes ½ cup sauce

1 tablespoon vegetable oil
4 chicken breast fillets (800g)
½ cup (125ml) dry white wine
2 tablespoons red wine vinegar
1 teaspoon white peppercorns, crushed
3 green onions, sliced thinly
1 sprig fresh thyme
1 dried bay leaf
2 sprigs fresh tarragon
1 cup (250ml) chicken stock
1 cup (250ml) water
50g cold butter, chopped

1 Heat oil in large frying pan; cook chicken, uncovered, until browned both sides and cooked through. Remove from pan; cover to keep warm.
2 Deglaze pan (see left) with wine, stirring, until mixture reduces by half. Add vinegar, peppercorn, onion and herbs; bring to a boil then reduce heat. Simmer, uncovered, about 3 minutes or until liquid has almost evaporated.
3 Add stock and the water; return to a boil then reduce heat. Simmer, uncovered, about 10 minutes or until sauce reduces to about ½ cup. Whisk in butter, piece by piece; strain sauce into small jug.
per serving 26.1g total fat (10.9g saturated fat); 1814kJ (434 cal); 1g carbohydrate; 43.8g protein; 0.2g fibre

cranberry and chive

preparation time 5 minutes cooking time 25 minutes
serves 4 makes 2 cups sauce

1 tablespoon olive oil
4 chicken breast fillets (800g)
⅓ cup (80ml) dry red wine
300g frozen cranberries
¾ cup (180ml) orange juice
¾ cup (180ml) water
1 tablespoon honey
2 tablespoons finely chopped fresh chives

1 Heat oil in large frying pan; cook chicken, uncovered, until browned both sides and cooked through. Remove from pan; cover to keep warm.
2 Deglaze pan (see left) with wine, stirring until mixture reduces by half. Add cranberries, juice and the water; bring to a boil then reduce heat. Simmer, uncovered, stirring occasionally, about 10 minutes or until sauce reduces by half. Stir honey and chives into sauce off the heat.
per serving 9.3g total fat (1.8g saturated fat); 1421kJ (340 cal); 12.3g carbohydrate; 45.9g protein; 1.7g fibre

tamarind soy

preparation time 5 minutes **cooking time** 10 minutes **makes** ½ cup

1 teaspoon peanut oil
1 clove garlic, crushed
2 tablespoons soy sauce
1 teaspoon brown sugar
2 tablespoons tamarind concentrate
2cm piece fresh ginger (10g), grated
⅓ cup (80ml) water
1 green onion, sliced thinly

1 Heat oil in small saucepan; cook garlic, stirring, until fragrant. Add sauce, sugar, tamarind, ginger and the water; bring to a boil then reduce heat. Simmer, uncovered, about 2 minutes or until sauce thickens. Stir in onion off the heat.

per tablespoon 0.8g total fat (0.1g saturated fat); 71kJ (17 cal); 1.8g carbohydrate; 0.5g protein; 0.3g fibre

makes enough for four 150g servings of pan-fried duck maryland.
also goes well with grilled chicken breast fillets; as a dipping sauce for grilled chicken wings.
commonly associated with the food of India and South-East Asia, tamarind is available dried and pressed into blocks or commercially produced as a paste or concentrate, which can be kept in the refrigerator indefinitely. It is used as a souring agent in pastes, sauces, marinades and dressings.

spiced yogurt

preparation time 5 minutes **cooking time** 5 minutes **makes** 1½ cups

1 teaspoon sweet paprika
1 teaspoon ground cinnamon
1 teaspoon ground coriander
1 teaspoon ground cumin
2 teaspoons fennel seeds
4cm piece fresh ginger (20g) grated
1 tablespoon sambal oelek
1¼ cups (350g) yogurt
1 tablespoon lemon juice

1 Dry-fry paprika, cinnamon, coriander, cumin and seeds in small frying pan, stirring over low heat until fragrant.
2 Combine roasted spices with ginger, sambal, yogurt and juice in small bowl.

per tablespoon 0.7g total fat (0.4g saturated fat); 67kJ (16 cal); 1.3g carbohydrate; 0.9g protein; 0.0g fibre

makes enough for six 210g servings of fried chicken drumettes.
tip Sauce can be made two days ahead and kept covered in the refrigerator.
also goes well with roasted potato wedges; grilled pork fillets or cutlets; smoked salmon.
paprika, from the Latin word for pepper, is the dried and ground form of a number of varieties of red capsicum. It is easily available from supermarkets in sweet, smoked or hot form, but there are as many as 12 different types found in specialist spice shops.

creamy pancetta, pea and tarragon

preparation time 15 minutes **cooking time** 15 minutes **makes** 1½ cups

makes enough for four 350g servings of roast chicken marylands.
tip Sauce should be served immediately after cooking.
also goes well with poached eggs or an omelette; potato mash; baked ham.
pancetta is an Italian unsmoked bacon; pork belly is cured in salt and spices then rolled into a sausage shape and dried for several weeks. It is most often used, either sliced or chopped, as an ingredient to add its flavour to recipes rather than eaten on its own.

1 tablespoon olive oil
2 shallots (50g), chopped finely
1 clove garlic, crushed
100g sliced pancetta, shredded finely
½ cup (125ml) dry white wine
300ml cream
½ cup (60g) frozen peas
1 tablespoon coarsely chopped fresh tarragon

1 Heat oil in large frying pan; cook shallot, garlic and pancetta, stirring, over medium heat until pancetta browns. Add wine; bring to a boil then reduce heat. Simmer, uncovered, about 2 minutes or until mixture reduces by half.
2 Add cream and peas; bring to a boil then reduce heat. Simmer, uncovered, 4 minutes, stirring occasionally. Add tarragon; simmer, uncovered, 2 minutes.

per tablespoon 9g total fat (5.2g saturated fat); 397kJ (95 cal);
0.9g carbohydrate; 1.6g protein; 0.2g fibre

spiced honey and coriander

preparation time 15 minutes **cooking time** 5 minutes **makes** ½ cup

makes enough sauce for four 150g servings of duck breasts.
also goes well with grilled pork fillets; barbecued pork spareribs; pan-fried chicken breast fillets.

20g butter
2cm piece fresh ginger (10g), grated
2 teaspoons finely grated orange rind
pinch ground clove
2 cardamom pods, bruised
½ teaspoon caraway seeds
⅓ cup (80ml) orange juice
¼ cup (90g) honey
¼ cup (60ml) chicken stock
2 teaspoons coarsely chopped fresh coriander

1 Melt butter in small frying pan; cook ginger, rind, clove, cardamom and seeds, stirring, until fragrant.
2 Stir in juice, honey and stock; bring to a boil then reduce heat. Simmer, uncovered, about 2 minutes or until mixture thickens slightly. Discard cardamom; stir in coriander off the heat.

per tablespoon 2.8g total fat (1.8g saturated fat); 330kJ (79 cal);
13.7g carbohydrate; 0.3g protein; 0.1g fibre

PASTA AND NOODLES ARE NOTHING WITHOUT A SAUCE. HERE IS A MOUTH-WATERING SAMPLE OF THE BEST OF THEM.

sauces for pasta

makes enough sauce for 500g pasta, to serve four people.
storage The sauce will keep, covered, under refrigeration for up to three days. Freeze sauce in sealed containers for up to three months.
cheat's way An equal quantity of canned diced tomatoes can be used instead of fresh tomatoes.
the name given to a dish usually denotes its place of origin or where it is usually cooked. Naples, the third most populous city in Italy, is synonymous with simple sauced pizza and spaghetti, and napoletana is the basis of many tomato-based sauces, four of which follow on page 51.

napoletana

preparation time 15 minutes **cooking time** 1 hour **makes** 4 cups

⅓ cup (80ml) olive oil
1 medium brown onion (150g), chopped finely
3 cloves garlic, crushed
¼ cup loosely packed fresh basil leaves
1 teaspoon sea salt
2 tablespoons tomato paste
1.5kg ripe tomatoes, chopped coarsely

1 Heat half of the oil in large saucepan; cook onion, garlic, basil and salt, stirring, until onion softens. Add paste; cook, stirring, 1 minute.
2 Add tomato; bring to a boil then reduce heat. Simmer, uncovered, stirring occasionally, about 45 minutes or until sauce thickens. Stir in remaining oil; simmer, uncovered, 5 minutes.
per tablespoon 1.6g total fat (0.2g saturated fat); 84kJ (20 cal);
0.9g carbohydrate; 0.4g protein; 0.5g fibre

Each of the following 4 pasta sauce recipes make enough for four servings (500g) of cooked pasta.

puttanesca

preparation time 20 minutes
cooking time 10 minutes **makes** 5 cups

4 whole anchovy fillets, drained
¼ cup (60ml) olive oil
1 fresh long red chilli, sliced thinly
1 litre (4 cups) napoletana sauce (page 48)
1 cup (120g) seeded black olives
2 tablespoons drained, rinsed baby capers,
   chopped coarsely

1 Finely chop anchovy fillets. Using side of heavy knife, press down firmly on anchovy to crush.
2 Heat 1 tablespoon of the oil in large saucepan; cook anchovy and chilli, stirring, 2 minutes. Add sauce; bring to a boil. Stir in olives, capers and remaining oil, reduce heat; simmer, uncovered, about 5 minutes or until heated through.
per tablespoon 2.2g total fat (0.3g saturated fat); 113kJ (27 cal); 1.2g carbohydrate; 0.4g protein; 0.4g fibre

arrabbiata

preparation time 15 minutes
cooking time 10 minutes **makes** 5 cups

¼ cup (60ml) olive oil
2 fresh small red thai chillies, chopped finely
1 litre (4 cups) napoletana sauce (page 48)
½ cup coarsely chopped fresh flat-leaf parsley

1 Heat half of the oil in large saucepan; cook chilli, stirring, 2 minutes. Add sauce; bring to a boil. Stir in remaining oil and parsley.
per tablespoon 2.2g total fat (0.3g saturated fat); 100kJ (24 cal); 0.7g carbohydrate; 0.3g protein; 0.4g fibre

amatriciana

preparation time 20 minutes
cooking time 15 minutes **makes** 5 cups

¼ cup (60ml) olive oil
200g pancetta, chopped finely
½ teaspoon dried chilli flakes
1 litre (4 cups) napoletana sauce (page 48)
⅓ cup (25g) finely grated parmesan
⅓ cup (25g) finely grated pecorino

1 Heat half the oil in large saucepan; cook pancetta, stirring, until browned. Add chilli and sauce; bring to a boil then reduce heat. Stir in remaining oil.
2 Combine cheeses with pasta sauce just before serving.
per tablespoon 2.9g total fat (0.6g saturated fat); 142kJ (34 cal); 0.7g carbohydrate; 1.2g protein; 0.4g fibre

marinara

preparation time 20 minutes
cooking time 15 minutes **makes** 5 cups

1 tablespoon olive oil
1 small brown onion (80g), chopped finely
2 tablespoons tomato paste
½ cup (125ml) dry white wine
1 litre (4 cups) napoletana sauce (page 48)
800g marinara mix
pinch saffron threads

1 Heat oil in large saucepan; cook onion, stirring, until soft. Add paste; cook, stirring, 1 minute. Add wine; bring to a boil then reduce heat. Simmer, uncovered, 3 minutes.
2 Add sauce, marinara mix and saffron; bring to a boil then reduce heat. Simmer, uncovered, about 5 minutes or until seafood is cooked through.
per tablespoon 1.8g total fat (0.3g saturated fat); 151kJ (36 cal); 1.5g carbohydrate; 2.9g protein; 0.5g fibre

vietnamese sweet, sour and spicy

preparation time 10 minutes **makes** 1 cup

¼ cup (60ml) water
¼ cup (60ml) fish sauce
¼ cup (60ml) rice vinegar
1½ tablespoons finely grated palm sugar
2 fresh small red thai chillies, chopped finely
2 tablespoons lime juice
2 tablespoons finely chopped fresh mint
2 tablespoons finely chopped fresh coriander

1 Combine ingredients in medium jug.

per tablespoon 0.0g total fat (0.0g saturated fat); 42kJ (10 cal); 1.9g carbohydrate; 0.5g protein; 0.1g fibre

makes enough sauce for four 250g servings of thin rice noodles.
also goes well with wontons; as a dipping sauce for spring or rice paper rolls.
storage Sauce will keep, covered, in the refrigerator, for up to three days in an airtight container.
a simple Vietnamese salad can consist of rice vermicelli, shredded barbecued chicken, coarsely chopped cooked prawns and a garnish of deep-fried shallots or finely chopped roasted peanuts.

peanut sambal

preparation time 15 minutes **cooking time** 10 minutes **makes** 2 cups

6 green onions
2 fresh small red thai chillies, chopped coarsely
2 tablespoons lime juice
1 tablespoon peanut oil
1 cup (140g) roasted salted peanuts
¼ teaspoon shrimp paste
410ml can coconut milk
1 tablespoon tamarind concentrate
2 teaspoons brown sugar

1 Finely chop two of the onions.
2 Quarter remaining four onions then blend or process with chilli, juice and half of the oil until chopped coarsely; add nuts, blend or process until mixture is chopped finely.
3 Heat remaining oil in medium frying pan; cook shrimp paste, stirring, about 1 minute or until fragrant. Add coconut milk, tamarind, sugar and processed onion mixture; bring to a boil then reduce heat. Simmer, uncovered, stirring occasionally, about 4 minutes or until sauce thickens slightly.
4 Stir in finely chopped onion off the heat.

per tablespoon 7.1g total fat (3.6g saturated fat); 330kJ (79 cal); 1.7g carbohydrate; 1.9g protein; 0.9g fibre

makes enough for four 125g servings of fried hokkien noodles.
tip If shrimp paste is unavailable, substitute 1 tablespoon fish sauce. Shrimp paste is available from Asian grocery stores or the Asian section of most supermarkets.
also goes well with stir-fried rice noodles; as a dipping sauce for raw vegetables.
tamarind concentrate is made from dried tamarind pulp and is a popular souring agent that adds an appetising tang and fruity background flavour to curries and sauces.

SAUCES FOR PASTA

pistachio and lemon pesto

preparation time 20 minutes **cooking time** 10 minutes **makes** 1½ cups

1 cup firmly packed fresh basil leaves
⅓ cup (45g) pistachios
⅓ cup (25g) coarsely grated parmesan
2 cloves garlic, quartered
1 tablespoon finely grated lemon rind
2 tablespoons lemon juice
½ cup (125ml) olive oil
½ cup (125ml) cream
1 tablespoon water

1 Blend or process basil, nuts, cheese, garlic, rind and juice until smooth. With motor operating, gradually add oil until pesto forms a smooth paste.
2 Combine pesto, cream and the water in medium frying pan; stir over medium heat until heated through.

per tablespoon 11.1g total fat (3.3g saturated fat); 443kJ (106 cal);
0.7g carbohydrate; 1.2g protein; 0.4g fibre

makes enough for four 125g servings of spaghetti.
tip Pesto, without the cream, will keep in the refrigerator for one week; cover with a film of oil. To freeze, place pesto in a sealed container. Because of its high oil content, pesto will never freeze solid, so you can use small amounts without defrosting the lot.
also goes well with grilled chicken breast fillets; pan-fried salmon steaks.
our spin on a typical "pesto alla Genovese" uses chopped pistachios instead of pine nuts and mixes in cream and lemon juice for "yum" value.

bolognese

preparation time 25 minutes **cooking time** 1 hour 45 minutes **makes** 8 cups

2 teaspoons olive oil
200g pancetta, chopped finely
1 medium brown onion (150g), chopped finely
1 small carrot (70g), chopped finely
2 trimmed celery stalks (200g), chopped finely
600g beef mince
½ cup (125ml) dry red wine
1 cup (250ml) beef stock
½ cup (140g) tomato paste
2 x 400g cans crushed tomatoes
½ cup coarsely chopped fresh flat-leaf parsley
2 tablespoons coarsely chopped fresh oregano

1 Heat oil in large heavy-based pan; cook pancetta, stirring, until crisp. Add onion, carrot and celery; cook, stirring, until vegetables soften. Add beef; cook, stirring occasionally, until beef just changes colour.
2 Add wine; bring to a boil then reduce heat. Simmer 5 minutes. Add stock, paste and undrained tomatoes; bring to a boil then reduce heat. Simmer, covered, 1 hour. Uncover; simmer about 30 minutes or until bolognese thickens. Stir in herbs off the heat.

per tablespoon 0.8g total fat (0.3g saturated fat); 79kJ (19 cal);
0.6g carbohydrate; 1.9g protein; 0.3g fibre

makes enough for eight 125g servings of spaghetti.
tip Try a combination of minces such as pork and veal, rather than just beef mince.
also goes well with lasagne; baked jacket potatoes; steamed rice.
bolognese is arguably the most well known of pasta sauces. Aromatic, hearty and full of flavour, this rich meat sauce remains a staple on dinner tables everywhere.

makes enough for four 125g servings of fettuccine.

tips For a lower-fat version, use light thickened cream. Parmigiano reggiano, a salty, sharp, aged cheese, is best used in this recipe, and is available at most delicatessens.

what went wrong Do not reduce the cream mixture too rapidly or by too much as this sauce can burn.

alfredo is named after Roman restaurateur Alfredo di Lello who is credited with creating this dish in the 1920s.

alfredo

preparation time 10 minutes **cooking time** 10 minutes **makes** 1 cup

80g butter
300ml cream
½ cup (40g) finely grated parmesan

1 Melt butter in medium frying pan. Add cream; bring to a boil then reduce heat. Simmer, uncovered, about 5 minutes or until sauce reduces by half.

2 Add cheese; stir over low heat about 2 minutes or until cheese melts.

per tablespoon 17.4g total fat (11.4g saturated fat); 681kJ (163 cal); 0.8g carbohydrate; 1.8g protein; 0.0g fibre

Each of the following 4 pasta sauce recipes make enough for four servings (500g) of cooked pasta.

carbonara

preparation time 10 minutes
cooking time 10 minutes **makes** 1 cup

60g butter
135g pancetta, sliced thinly
1 clove garlic, crushed
1 teaspoon cracked black pepper
300ml cream
2 eggs, beaten lightly
½ cup (40g) finely grated parmesan
½ cup (40g) finely grated romano

1 Melt butter in medium frying pan; cook pancetta, stirring, 5 minutes. Add garlic, pepper and cream; simmer, uncovered until sauce reduces by half. Remove from heat.
2 Stir in egg and cheeses.

per tablespoon 19.3g total fat (12.0g saturated fat); 832kJ (199 cal); 0.8g carbohydrate; 6.1g protein; 0.0g fibre

boscaiola

preparation time 10 minutes
cooking time 10 minutes **makes** 1 cup

60g butter
135g pancetta, chopped finely
150g mushrooms, sliced thinly
1 clove garlic, crushed
1 teaspoon cracked black pepper
300ml cream
½ cup (40g) finely grated parmesan

1 Melt butter in medium frying pan; cook pancetta, stirring, 5 minutes. Add mushrooms and garlic; cook, stirring, 3 minutes.
2 Add pepper and cream; simmer, uncovered, about 5 minutes or until sauce reduces by half.
3 Add cheese; stir over low heat, about 2 minutes or until cheese melts.

per tablespoon 17.6g total fat (11.1g saturated fat); 740kJ (177 cal); 1g carbohydrate; 4.4g protein; 0.4g fibre

tomato, chilli and cream

preparation time 10 minutes
cooking time 10 minutes **makes** 1 cup

60g butter
1 small brown onion (80g), chopped finely
1 cup (150g) drained semi-dried tomatoes, chopped coarsely
½ teaspoon dried chilli flakes
2 cloves garlic, crushed
1 teaspoon cracked black pepper
300ml cream
½ cup (40g) finely grated parmesan

1 Melt butter in medium frying pan; cook onion, stirring, until soft. Add tomato, chilli and garlic; cook, stirring, 3 minutes.
2 Add pepper and cream; simmer, uncovered, 5 minutes or until sauce reduces by half.
3 Add cheese; stir over low heat about 2 minutes or until cheese melts.

per tablespoon 16.6g total fat (10.6g saturated fat); 777kJ (186 cal); 5.6g carbohydrate; 3.3g protein; 2g fibre

quattro formaggi

preparation time 5 minutes
cooking time 10 minutes **makes** 1½ cups

50g butter
300ml cream
50g gorgonzola, crumbled
1 cup (80g) finely grated pecorino
½ cup (50g) finely grated fontina
1 cup (80g) finely grated parmesan

1 Melt butter in medium frying pan, add cream; bring to a boil then reduce heat. Simmer, uncovered, about 5 minutes or until mixture reduces by half.
2 Remove pan from heat; add cheeses gradually, stirring, until sauce is almost smooth.
tip Different cheeses can be used if the ones mentioned are unavailable. Gruyère, mozzarella, mild brie blue, provolone, vintage cheddar or raclette – mix and match until you find a combination you like best.

per tablespoon 13.9g total fat (9.1g saturated fat); 598kJ (143 cal); 0.5g carbohydrate; 4.6g protein; 0.0g fibre

MEAT MAY BE
BIG IN FLAVOUR
ALREADY, BUT
SERVING IT WITH
A SAUCE WILL
ADD SUBTLETY
AND REFINEMENT.

sauces for meat

beef

makes enough for six 125g servings of roast beef.

tip If the sauce is too thick, add a little extra hot water.

also goes well with standing rib roast, roasted potato wedges; grilled chicken breasts.

horseradish, a strong-flavoured member of the mustard family, is sold in various forms: be certain to use the prepared version here rather than horseradish cream.

horseradish

preparation time 10 minutes **cooking time** 10 minutes **makes** 1½ cups

2 teaspoons olive oil
2 green onions, chopped finely
¼ cup (60ml) dry white wine
¼ cup (70g) prepared horseradish
300g sour cream
2 tablespoons lemon juice
1 teaspoon dijon mustard
2 teaspoons finely chopped fresh dill
2 tablespoons hot water

1 Heat oil in medium frying pan; cook onion, stirring, until soft. Add wine; bring to a boil then reduce heat. Simmer, uncovered, until liquid has almost evaporated.

2 Add horseradish, sour cream, juice and mustard; cook, stirring, until sauce is heated through. Stir in dill and the hot water off the heat.

per tablespoon 7.2g total fat (4.2g saturated fat); 305kJ (73 cal); 1g carbohydrate; 0.6g protein; 0.3g fibre

tangy barbecue

preparation time 5 minutes **cooking time** 25 minutes **makes** 2 cups

1 cup (250ml) tomato sauce
½ cup (125ml) apple cider vinegar
¼ cup (60ml) worcestershire sauce
⅔ cup (150g) firmly packed brown sugar
2 tablespoons american-style mustard
1 fresh small red thai chilli, chopped finely
1 clove garlic, crushed
1 tablespoon lemon juice

1 Combine ingredients in medium saucepan; bring to a boil then reduce heat. Simmer, uncovered, stirring occasionally, 20 minutes.
per tablespoon 0.1g total fat (0.0g saturated fat); 163kJ (39 cal); 9.3g carbohydrate; 0.3g protein; 0.3g fibre

makes enough for six beefburgers or 2kg of braised short ribs.
tip This sauce is best made a day in advance. Keep, under refrigeration, for up to three days in a screw-top jar.
also goes well with roasted potato wedges; as a sauce for home-made baked beans.

chinese black bean

preparation time 5 minutes **cooking time** 5 minutes **makes** 1 cup

1 tablespoon peanut oil
1 teaspoon sesame oil
1 green onion, sliced thinly
2cm piece fresh ginger (10g), grated
1 clove garlic, crushed
2 tablespoons salted black beans, rinsed, drained, crushed
¼ cup (60ml) soy sauce
2 teaspoons brown sugar
1 tablespoon cornflour
¾ cup (180ml) water

1 Heat oils in wok; stir-fry onion, ginger, garlic and beans until mixture is fragrant.
2 Add sauce and sugar to wok; cook, stirring, 1 minute. Add blended cornflour and the water; cook, stirring, until sauce boils and thickens.
per tablespoon 3.1g total fat (0.5g saturated fat); 176kJ (42 cal); 2.5g carbohydrate; 0.9g protein; 0.4g fibre

makes enough for four 200g servings of beef strips in a stir-fry.
also goes well with steamed crab; par-boiled green vegetables.
salted black beans, available from all Asian food stores, are soft and chewy fermented soy beans having a pungent aroma and adding a distinct flavour to food.

deglazing beef

tips For a sweeter version of this sauce, omit the fresh ginger and double the amount of glacé ginger. If you want the sauce to be smoother, push through a fine sieve into a small bowl then discard solids.
goes well with stir-fried vegetables or noodles; pan-fried scallops.

deglazing is the initial step in making a sauce that incorporates the browned bits sticking to the bottom of a pan in which meat has been cooked. A small amount of liquid is added to any remaining meat juices in the pan, then over heat, the pan is scraped to loosen the browned caramelised bits. After the mixture is combined, flour is often stirred in to make a roux-like base for the sauce; other times, cream or butter will be added to create a richer, more velvety sauce.

tip As the sauce is heated, the alcohol can ignite. It generally burns off in a matter of seconds, but shaking the pan will extinguish the flame. Keep a lid nearby, exercise caution and don't use your exhaust fan when making this sauce.
also goes well with pan-fried veal steaks; roasted kangaroo.

zesty three-ginger

preparation time 5 minutes **cooking time** 15 minutes
serves 4 **makes** 1 cup sauce

1 tablespoon olive oil
20g butter
4 beef eye-fillet steaks (600g)
1 small brown onion (80g), chopped coarsely
2cm piece fresh ginger (10g), grated
1 tablespoon finely chopped glacé ginger
½ cup (125ml) green ginger wine
1 tablespoon plain flour
1 cup (250ml) beef stock

1 Heat half of the oil and half of the butter in medium frying pan; cook beef, uncovered, until cooked as desired. Remove from pan; cover to keep warm.
2 Heat remaining oil and butter in same pan; cook onion and both gingers, stirring, until onion softens.
3 Deglaze pan (see left) with wine. Add flour; cook, stirring about 2 minutes or until mixture bubbles and thickens.
4 Gradually add stock; bring to a boil then reduce heat. Simmer, uncovered, about 5 minutes or until mixture boils and thickens slightly.
per serving 17.8g total fat (7.2g saturated fat); 1417kJ (339 cal);
5.5g carbohydrate; 33.1g protein; 0.5g fibre

sauce diane

preparation time 5 minutes **cooking time** 15 minutes
serves 4 **makes** 1 cup sauce

1 tablespoon olive oil
4 New York-cut steaks (880g)
⅓ cup (80ml) brandy
1 clove garlic, crushed
¼ cup (60ml) worcestershire sauce
2 teaspoons dijon mustard
300ml cream

1 Heat oil in large frying pan; cook beef, uncovered, until cooked as desired. Remove from pan; cover to keep warm.
2 Deglaze pan (see left) with brandy, stirring until mixture bubbles and starts to thicken.
3 Add remaining ingredients; bring to a boil then reduce heat. Simmer, uncovered, about 5 minutes or until sauce thickens slightly.
per serving 50.1g total fat (27.6g saturated fat); 2926kJ (700 cal);
5.6g carbohydrate; 48.4g protein; 0.3g fibre

SAUCES FOR MEAT

caramelised red onion

preparation time 15 minutes **cooking time** 40 minutes **makes** 1½ cups

50g butter
4 medium red onions (680g), sliced thinly
1 tablespoon brown sugar
⅓ cup (80ml) dry red wine
¼ cup (60ml) beef stock
1 tablespoon balsamic vinegar

1 Melt butter in large frying pan; cook onion over low heat, stirring occasionally, about 30 minutes.

2 Add sugar; cook, stirring, about 5 minutes or until onion has caramelised. Add wine, stock and vinegar; bring to a boil then remove from heat.

per tablespoon 2.3g total fat (1.5g saturated fat); 159kJ (38 cal); 2.8g carbohydrate; 0.6g protein; 0.5g fibre

makes enough for six 200g servings of grilled sirloin steak. **tip** Substitute brown onions for the red ones. **also goes well with** grilled chicken; barbecued swordfish; vegetarian quiche. **what went wrong** If the onion browns too much at the first stage of cooking, reduce the heat. **caramelising** food breaks down its natural sugars, causing a concentration of flavour that gives its sweet taste.

bordelaise

preparation time 10 minutes **cooking time** 1 hour 25 minutes **makes** ½ cup

3 green onions, chopped coarsely
½ teaspoon dried green peppercorns, crushed
2 cups (500ml) dry red wine
1½ cups (375ml) beef stock
1 sprig fresh thyme
2 dried bay leaves
2 stalks fresh flat-leaf parsley
60g cold unsalted butter, chopped

1 Combine onion, pepper and wine in medium saucepan; bring to a boil then reduce heat. Simmer, uncovered, about 15 minutes or until reduced by a third.

2 Add stock, thyme, bay leaves and parsley; bring to a boil then reduce heat. Simmer, uncovered, about 1 hour or until sauce is reduced to ½ cup. Strain, discard herbs.

3 Return sauce to same cleaned pan; stir in butter, piece by piece, over low heat, until sauce is smooth.

per tablespoon 8.3g total fat (5.5g saturated fat); 568kJ (136 cal); 0.7g carbohydrate; 1.1g protein; 0.1g fibre

makes enough for four 125g servings of grilled veal cutlets. **also goes well with** roast lamb backstraps; fried pork fillets. **what went wrong** If the sauce is too thin, it has not been reduced sufficiently; return to heat before adding the butter. **traditionally** made with beef marrow, bordelaise has its origins in France in the Bordeaux region.

beef

makes enough for
four 200g servings
of pan-fried veal cutlets.
tip Substitute thinly sliced
swiss brown mushrooms,
if porcini are unavailable.
also goes well with
pan-fried beef eye fillets;
roasted lamb backstraps;
grilled chicken thigh cutlets.
porcini, also known as
cèpes, are large-topped,
meaty mushrooms,
mostly sold dried but
also found fresh.

porcini, marsala and rosemary

preparation time 5 minutes (plus standing time)
cooking time 5 minutes **makes** 1 cup

5g dried porcini mushrooms
20g butter
1 shallot (25g), chopped finely
1 tablespoon fresh rosemary leaves
¼ cup (60ml) marsala
½ cup (125ml) cream

1 Place mushrooms in small heatproof bowl, cover with boiling water, stand
20 minutes; drain. Discard stems; slice caps thinly.
2 Melt butter in small frying pan; cook shallot, stirring, until soft. Add mushrooms,
rosemary and marsala; bring to a boil then reduce heat. Simmer, uncovered,
3 minutes.
3 Add cream; bring to a boil then reduce heat. Simmer, uncovered, about
3 minutes or until sauce reduces by half.
per tablespoon 5.9g total fat (3.9g saturated fat); 259kJ (62 cal);
1g carbohydrate; 0.3g protein; 0.0g fibre

makes enough for four
150g servings of pan-
fried veal scaloppine.
also goes well with
grilled chicken breast
fillets; barbecued pork
medallions; roasted
lamb cutlets.
marsala, a caramel-
flavoured fortified wine,
is named after the city
from which it comes,
and is the most popular
dessert wine in Italy. Dry
marsala is often served
as an apéritif.

marsala

preparation time 5 minutes **cooking time** 10 minutes **makes** ½ cup

20g butter
2 shallots (50g), chopped finely
2 teaspoons plain flour
½ cup (125ml) marsala
½ cup (125ml) beef stock

1 Melt butter in small frying pan; cook shallot, stirring, until soft. Add flour; cook,
stirring, 2 minutes.
2 Stir in marsala; bring to a boil then reduce heat. Simmer, uncovered, 2 minutes.
Add stock; bring to a boil then reduce heat. Simmer, uncovered, about 4 minutes
or until sauce has reduced by half.
per serving 0.9g total fat (0.6g saturated fat); 63kJ (15 cal); 0.7g carbohydrate;
0.1g protein; 0.0g fibre

lamb

spinach and crème fraîche

preparation time 5 minutes **cooking time** 10 minutes **makes** 1½ cups

makes enough for six
200g servings of grilled
lamb forequarter chops.
tip Do not allow
crème fraîche to boil
or it will separate.
also goes well with
barbecued beef fillet
steaks; grilled chicken
breast fillets; crumbed
fish cutlets.
crème fraîche has a
thick consistency and
tangy flavour. It is similar
to sour cream, but has a
higher butterfat content.

30g butter
2 cloves garlic, crushed
6 shallots (150g), chopped finely
2 teaspoons dijon mustard
100g baby spinach leaves
1 cup (240g) crème fraîche

1 Melt butter in large frying pan; cook garlic and shallot, stirring, about 5 minutes
or until shallot softens.
2 Add mustard and spinach; cook, stirring, until spinach wilts. Add crème fraîche;
cook, stirring, over low heat, until just heated through.
per tablespoon 6.7g total fat (4.4g saturated fat); 272kJ (65 cal);
0.7g carbohydrate; 0.6g protein; 0.3g fibre

mint

preparation time 5 minutes **cooking time** 5 minutes (plus standing time)
makes 1 cup

makes enough for a
2kg roast leg of lamb.
also goes well with
felafel; mixed bean
or rice salad.
mint sauce is a classic
accompaniment to a
traditional roast: it is said
ancient Romans would
sprinkle their tables with
mint leaves before a feast
because it was thought
the aroma prepared the
mind for eating meat.

2 cups firmly packed fresh mint leaves
¼ cup (60ml) water
¾ cup (180ml) white wine vinegar
2 tablespoons caster sugar

1 Chop half of the mint coarsely; place in small heatproof bowl.
2 Combine the water, vinegar and sugar in small saucepan; stir over heat,
without boiling, until sugar dissolves. Pour liquid over chopped mint in bowl,
cover; stand 3 hours.
3 Strain liquid into bowl; discard mint. Chop remaining mint coarsely; stir into
liquid. Blend or process until chopped finely.
per tablespoon 0.3g total fat (0.1g saturated fat); 234kJ (56 cal);
10.1g carbohydrate; 0.9g protein; 1.9g fibre

SAUCES FOR MEAT

skordalia

preparation time 5 minutes (plus standing time) **cooking time** 15 minutes
makes 1 cup

1 medium potato (200g), quartered
3 cloves garlic, quartered
2 tablespoons cold water
1 tablespoon lemon juice
1 tablespoon white wine vinegar
⅓ cup (80ml) olive oil

1 Boil, steam or microwave potato until tender; drain. Cool 10 minutes.
2 Blend or process potato, garlic, the water, juice and vinegar until mixture is pureed. With motor operating, gradually add oil in thin, steady stream, processing until mixture thickens.

per tablespoon 6.1g total fat (0.9g saturated fat); 280kJ (67 cal); 2.3g carbohydrate; 0.5g protein; 0.4g fibre

makes enough for four servings of lamb kebabs.
tip If skordalia is too thick, add small amounts of hot water until the desired consistency is reached.
also goes well with fried zucchini and eggplant strips; battered fish; grilled chicken breasts.
skordalia, a Greek sauce or dip, can be made with breadcrumbs or pureed potato – but always with garlic.

semi-dried tomato

preparation time 10 minutes **cooking time** 20 minutes **makes** 1½ cups

2 teaspoons olive oil
1 medium brown onion (150g), chopped finely
2 cloves garlic, crushed
1 tablespoon tomato paste
1 cup (150g) drained semi-dried tomatoes, chopped coarsely
1½ cups (375ml) water
¼ cup finely chopped fresh flat-leaf parsley

1 Heat oil in large saucepan; cook onion and garlic, stirring, about 5 minutes or until onion softens. Add paste; cook, stirring, 2 minutes. Add tomato and the water; bring to a boil then reduce heat. Simmer, uncovered, about 5 minutes or until sauce thickens slightly.
2 Blend or process mixture until smooth. Stir in parsley.

per tablespoon 0.9g total fat (0.1g saturated fat); 125kJ (30 cal); 3.6g carbohydrate; 1.1g protein; 1.5g fibre

makes enough for six 200g servings of pan-fried lamb backstraps.
tip Semi-dried tomatoes bought by weight from a delicatessen are best for this recipe. If you use those sold packaged in oil, drain well and pat with absorbent paper before use.
also goes well with grilled sirloin steaks; grilled pork cutlets; pan-fried chicken breasts.

deglazing lamb

tip Substitute cashews for pistachios if you like.
also goes well with pan-fried white fish fillets; grilled beef fillets.

deglazing is the initial step in making a sauce that incorporates the browned bits sticking to the bottom of a pan in which meat has been cooked. A small amount of liquid is added to any remaining meat juices in the pan, then over heat, the pan is scraped to loosen the browned caramelised bits. After the mixture is combined, flour is often stirred in to make a roux-like base for the sauce; other times, cream or butter will be added to create a richer, more velvety sauce.

tip For a less tangy sauce, reduce the amount of lemon juice.
also goes well with pan-fried white fish fillets; pan-fried beef fillet.

moroccan-spiced apricot and pistachio

preparation time 15 minutes cooking time 10 minutes
serves 4 makes 1 cup sauce

1 tablespoon olive oil
600g lamb backstraps
¾ cup (180ml) dry white wine
1½ cups (375ml) chicken stock
½ cup (75g) thinly sliced dried apricots
2cm piece fresh ginger (10g), grated
1 teaspoon coriander seeds, crushed
¼ teaspoon ground cumin
¼ teaspoon ground chilli
1 teaspoon ground cinnamon
2 tablespoons coarsely chopped pistachios
2 tablespoons coarsely chopped fresh flat-leaf parsley
30g cold butter, chopped

1 Heat oil in large frying pan; cook lamb, in batches, until cooked as desired.
2 Deglaze pan (see left) with wine; simmer 1 minute. Add stock, apricot and ginger; bring to a boil. Simmer, stirring occasionally, until liquid reduces by half.
3 Dry-fry coriander, cumin, chilli and cinnamon in small frying pan until fragrant.
4 Stir spices, nuts and parsley into apricot mixture. Add butter, piece by piece, whisking constantly until butter is melted and sauce thickens slightly.
per serving 26.9g total fat (11.2g saturated fat); 1881kJ (450 cal);
10.1g carbohydrate; 34.4g protein; 2.3g fibre

lemon, artichoke and thyme

preparation time 10 minutes cooking time 20 minutes
serves 4 makes 2 cups sauce

30g butter
2 tablespoons plain flour
1 cup (250ml) chicken stock
1 tablespoon olive oil
600g lamb backstraps
½ cup (125ml) dry white wine
2 teaspoons finely grated lemon rind
¼ cup (60ml) lemon juice
100g drained artichoke hearts, quartered
2 teaspoons finely chopped fresh thyme
½ cup (125ml) cream

1 Heat butter in small saucepan; add flour, cook, stirring, until mixture bubbles and thickens. Gradually add stock; stirring, until mixture boils and thickens.
2 Heat oil in large frying pan; cook lamb, in batches, until cooked as desired.
3 Deglaze pan (see left) with wine, add stock mixture, rind, juice, artichoke, thyme and cream; bring to a boil. Simmer about 5 minutes or until sauce thickens slightly.
per serving 38.3g total fat (19.9g saturated fat); 2195kJ (525 cal);
6.4g carbohydrate; 33.9g protein; 0.3g fibre

pork

makes enough for
1.5kg american-style
pork spareribs.
tip Ribs can be marinated
in the sauce for three
hours or overnight; use
the marinade to baste
ribs during cooking.
also goes well with
grilled pork cutlets;
as a marinade for
chicken wings.
hoisin is a thick, sweet
chinese barbecue sauce
made from salted
fermented soy beans,
onions and garlic. It can
be used in marinades, for
a baste, as a glaze, and
as an ingredient in dipping
sauces, stir-fries, braises
or roasted dishes.

makes 16 pork satay
sticks, enough to serve
four people.
tips Brush pork with a
mixture of chilli, garlic,
spices and oil, cover;
refrigerate for 3 hours
or overnight. Soak
bamboo skewers in
water for at least an hour
to prevent them from
splintering or scorching
during cooking.
also goes well with
grilled chicken breasts;
cold mixed steamed
vegetables; vegetable
or tofu skewers.
throughout Indonesia
and Malaya, marinated
then grilled meat, poultry
or fish skewers served
with a spicy peanut
sauce are a mainstay
for snacks as well as
main meals.

hoisin and peanut dipping

preparation time 5 minutes **cooking time** 10 minutes **makes** 1 cup

1 tablespoon caster sugar
2 tablespoons rice vinegar
½ cup (125ml) water
½ cup (125ml) hoisin sauce
2 tablespoons crushed unsalted peanuts, roasted

1 Combine sugar, vinegar and the water in small saucepan; stir over heat until sugar dissolves.
2 Add sauce; bring to a boil then reduce heat. Simmer, uncovered, about 5 minutes or until thickened slightly. Stir nuts into sauce off the heat.
per tablespoon 1.5g total fat (0.2g saturated fat); 171kJ (41 cal); 5.7g carbohydrate; 0.7g protein; 1.3g fibre

satay

preparation time 5 minutes **cooking time** 5 minutes **makes** 1 cup

⅓ cup (95g) crunchy peanut butter
1 fresh long red chilli, chopped finely
140ml can coconut milk
2 teaspoons fish sauce
2 teaspoons kecap manis
1 tablespoon lime juice

1 Combine ingredients in small saucepan; cook, stirring, over low heat until heated through.
per tablespoon 6.4g total fat (2.8g saturated fat); 309kJ (74 cal); 1.3g carbohydrate; 2.5g protein; 1.1g fibre

maple, bourbon and pear

preparation time 10 minutes **cooking time** 15 minutes
serves 4 **makes** 1½ cups sauce

20g butter
2 teaspoons olive oil
4 pork cutlets (950g)
1 large pear (330g), sliced thinly
¼ cup (60ml) bourbon
2 tablespoons maple syrup
½ cup (125ml) chicken stock
1 teaspoon lemon juice
½ cup (50g) coarsely chopped walnuts, roasted

1 Heat butter and oil in large frying pan; cook pork, in batches, until browned both sides and cooked as desired. Cover to keep warm.
2 Cook pear in same pan, turning gently, until browned and softened.
3 Deglaze pan (see right) with bourbon. Simmer 1 minute.
4 Add remaining ingredients; bring to a boil. Boil, uncovered, about 3 minutes or until sauce thickens slightly.

per serving 31.9g total fat (9.3g saturated fat); 2174kJ (520 cal); 20.4g carbohydrate; 30.7g protein; 2.3g fibre

charcuterie

preparation time 10 minutes **cooking time** 25 minutes
serves 4 **makes** 1 cup sauce

1 tablespoon olive oil
4 pork cutlets (950g)
1 small brown onion (80g), chopped finely
2 bacon rashers (140g), rind removed, sliced thinly
⅔ cup (160ml) dry white wine
⅔ cup (160ml) chicken stock
⅓ cup (60g) cornichons, sliced thinly lengthways
⅓ cup (40g) seeded green olives, sliced thinly
2 teaspoons dijon mustard
2 tablespoons finely chopped fresh flat-leaf parsley

1 Heat oil in large frying pan; cook pork, in batches, until browned both sides and cooked as desired. Cover to keep warm.
2 Add onion and bacon to pan; cook, stirring, until onion softens.
3 Deglaze pan (see right) with wine, stirring until mixture reduces by half.
4 Stir in remaining ingredients; bring to a boil. Boil, uncovered, about 1 minute or until sauce thickens slightly.

per serving 24.1g total fat (7.4g saturated fat); 1697kJ (406 cal); 7.7g carbohydrate; 33g protein; 0.9g fibre

---

deglazing pork

tip Pecans can be substituted for the walnuts to give a slightly different flavour. **also goes well with** pan-fried chicken or duck breasts; turkey steaks; pork loin chops.

deglazing is the initial step in making a sauce that incorporates the browned bits sticking to the bottom of a pan in which meat has been cooked. A small amount of liquid is added to any remaining meat juices in the pan, then over heat, the pan is scraped to loosen the browned caramelised bits. After the mixture is combined, flour is often stirred in to make a roux-like base for the sauce; other times, cream or butter will be added to create a richer, more velvety sauce.

also goes well with grilled pork sausages; barbecued veal steaks; pan-fried chicken breasts.

pork

makes enough for
four 200g servings
of pan-fried pork cutlets.
tip Barely ripe figs are
best to use here; if
overripe, they are likely to
fall apart during cooking.
The best way to store
fresh figs is in an egg
carton just loosely closed.
also goes well with
grilled chicken breast
fillets; pan-fried firm
white fish fillets.
fresh figs are best suited
to this recipe but, out of
season, dried turkish or
greek figs are suitable.
Figs go well with pork
and wild game, and
they give a unique flavour
and sweet undertone
to a dish.

caramelised spiced fig syrup

preparation time 10 minutes cooking time 20 minutes makes 1 cup

30g butter
6 small fresh figs (210g), quartered
3cm piece fresh ginger (15g), sliced thinly
2 star anise
2 tablespoons brown sugar
¼ cup (60ml) port
½ cup (125ml) chicken stock
½ cup (125ml) water

1 Melt butter over medium heat in medium frying pan; cook figs, ginger and star anise, stirring, about 5 minutes or until figs are caramelised. Remove figs from pan.
2 Add sugar, port, stock and the water to pan; bring to a boil then reduce heat. Simmer, stirring occasionally, about 10 minutes or until mixture reduces by half. Return figs to pan; simmer, uncovered, 1 minute.
per tablespoon 2.1g total fat (1.4g saturated fat); 176kJ (42 cal); 4.2g carbohydrate; 0.4g protein; 0.4g fibre

makes enough for
four 200g servings
of pan-fried pork cutlets.
also goes well with
deep-fried chicken
drumsticks; roasted
lamb backstraps;
roasted pork loin.

mustard and basil cream

preparation time 5 minutes cooking time 10 minutes makes 1 cup

2 teaspoons olive oil
1 clove garlic, crushed
¼ cup (60ml) dry white wine
300ml cream
1 tablespoon dijon mustard
¼ cup finely chopped fresh basil

1 Heat oil in small frying pan; cook garlic, stirring, until fragrant. Add wine; bring to a boil then reduce heat. Simmer, uncovered, until liquid reduces by half.
2 Add cream and mustard; cook, stirring, until sauce thickens and reduces to about a cup. Remove from heat; stir basil into sauce.
per tablespoon 11.6g total fat (7.3g saturated fat); 468kJ (112 cal); 0.8g carbohydrate; 0.6g protein; 0.1g fibre

NOTHING LIVENS
UP A VEGETABLE
DISH SO MUCH
AS A SAUCE – IT
CAN TURN WHAT
WOULD HAVE
BEEN A SIMPLE
VEGETABLE DISH
INTO AN ELEGANT
FIRST COURSE.

sauces for vegetables

hot and sour peanut

preparation time 5 minutes cooking time 15 minutes (plus cooling time)
makes 2 cups

makes enough to accompany 500g of grilled or roasted mixed vegetables.
tip Stir ¼ cup hot water into sauce to thin it, if desired.
also goes well with grilled chicken tenderloins; fish or beef skewers; roasted eggplant; stirred into a filling for fresh spring rolls.

1 tablespoon peanut oil
1 medium brown onion (150g), chopped coarsely
1 clove garlic, crushed
1 fresh small red thai chilli, chopped finely
⅔ cup (90g) unsalted peanuts, roasted
1 tablespoon lime juice
1 tablespoon brown sugar
1 tablespoon tamarind concentrate
1 tablespoon kecap manis
4cm piece fresh ginger (20g), grated
270ml can coconut milk

1 Heat oil in medium saucepan; cook onion, garlic and chilli, stirring, until onion softens.
2 Add remaining ingredients; bring mixture to a boil then reduce heat. Simmer, uncovered, 5 minutes. Cool to room temperature.
3 Blend or process until mixture forms a slightly chunky sauce.
per tablespoon 4.9g total fat (2.4g saturated fat); 238kJ (57 cal); 1.8g carbohydrate; 1.3g protein; 0.6g fibre

SAUCES FOR VEGETABLES

rice wine and soy

preparation time 5 minutes cooking time 10 minutes makes 1 cup

1 tablespoon peanut oil
2 teaspoons sesame oil
2 cloves garlic, crushed
5cm piece fresh ginger (25g), grated
1 green onion, sliced thinly
¼ cup (60ml) rice wine
2 tablespoons soy sauce
2 teaspoons caster sugar
1 teaspoon cornflour
½ cup (125ml) water

1 Heat oils in wok; stir-fry garlic, ginger and onion until fragrant. Add wine, sauce and sugar; bring to a boil then reduce heat. Simmer, uncovered, 2 minutes.
2 Add blended cornflour and the water; cook, stirring, until mixture comes to a boil and thickens slightly.
per tablespoon 2.3g total fat (0.4g saturated fat); 134kJ (32 cal); 1.4g carbohydrate; 0.3g protein; 0.2g fibre

makes enough sauce to accompany 500g grilled baby bok choy. **also goes well with** steamed broccoli; stir-fried beef strips.

capsicum sabayon

preparation time 5 minutes cooking time 25 minutes makes 1 cup

1 medium red capsicum (200g), chopped coarsely
1 cup (250ml) chicken stock
1 sprig fresh thyme
4 egg yolks
60g cold unsalted butter, chopped

1 Combine capsicum, stock and thyme in small saucepan; bring to a boil then reduce heat. Simmer, uncovered, 15 minutes. Discard thyme.
2 Blend or process capsicum mixture until smooth. Strain into medium bowl set over medium saucepan of simmering water. Add egg yolks; whisk about 7 minutes or until sauce thickens. Stir butter, piece by piece, into sauce.
per tablespoon 5.8g total fat (3.2g saturated fat); 251kJ (60 cal); 0.8g carbohydrate; 1.4g protein; 0.2g fibre

tip Warm sabayon must be served immediately. **goes well with** roasted potato wedges; deep-fried cauliflower; steamed broccoli or broccolini.

fennel and pernod

preparation time 10 minutes cooking time 20 minutes **makes** 2 cups

makes enough to
accompany six servings
of steamed asparagus.
also goes well with
steamed artichokes;
grilled lobster; stirred
through mashed
potatoes; tossed
into seafood pasta.

1 small fennel bulb (200g)
20g butter
1 tablespoon olive oil
¼ teaspoon fennel seeds
1 teaspoon cumin seeds
¼ cup (60ml) pernod
¾ cup (180g) cream
1 teaspoon lemon juice

1 Using sharp knife, mandoline or V-slicer, slice fennel thinly.
2 Melt butter and oil in medium frying pan; cook fennel and seeds over
low heat, uncovered, until fennel softens.
3 Add pernod; bring to a boil then reduce heat, simmer 1 minute.
4 Add cream and juice; bring to a boil then reduce heat, simmer
about 2 minutes or until sauce thickens slightly.
per tablespoon 4.7g total fat (2.7g saturated fat); 230kJ (55 cal);
1.6g carbohydrate; 0.2g protein; 1.1g fibre

sun-dried tomato mayonnaise

preparation time 20 minutes **makes** 1 cup

makes enough for four
500g servings of roasted
potato wedges.
also goes well with
chicken burger with the
lot; corn fritters; as a
sandwich filling; as a dip
for fresh vegetables.
what went wrong Oil
needs to be added
slowly to prevent mixture
separating. Should the
mixture separate, whisk
in two tablespoons of
hot water.

2 egg yolks
½ teaspoon salt
¾ teaspoon dry mustard
⅔ cup (160ml) extra light olive oil
2 tablespoons olive oil
2 tablespoons sun-dried tomato oil
1 tablespoon finely chopped drained sun-dried tomatoes
2 tablespoons hot water
1 tablespoon white vinegar

1 Combine egg yolks, salt and mustard in medium bowl. Gradually add
combined oils, in thin, steady stream, whisking constantly until mixture thickens.
2 Add tomato and the water; whisk until combined. Stir in vinegar.
per tablespoon 19.2g total fat (2.8g saturated fat); 723kJ (173 cal);
0.3g carbohydrate; 0.6g protein; 0.1g fibre

SAUCES FOR VEGETABLES

taratoor

preparation time 5 minutes **makes** 1 cup

½ cup (140g) tahini
2 cloves garlic, crushed
½ cup (125ml) hot water
⅓ cup lemon juice

1 Combine ingredients in small bowl.
per tablespoon 7.1g total fat (0.9g saturated fat); 326kJ (78 cal);
0.4g carbohydrate; 2.5g protein; 1.7g fibre

makes enough to accompany 500g of roasted eggplant.
tip Add a tablespoon of fresh chopped parsley or a little ground chilli or cumin to vary the flavour. Sauce is best served immediately if fresh herbs are used.
also goes well with oven-roasted or barbecued whole fish; felafels; as an addition to salad sandwiches or pitta pockets.
taratoor is a sauce using tahini, a thick paste made from ground sesame seeds and used in such dishes as hummus and baba ghanoush. Because it tends to settle into layers, tahini needs to be stirred thoroughly before it's measured.

red lentil and lemon grass

preparation time 15 minutes **cooking time** 20 minutes **makes** 2 cups

½ cup (100g) red lentils
1 small white onion (80g), chopped coarsely
2 cups (500ml) water
2 teaspoons olive oil
2 cloves garlic, crushed
1 fresh long red chilli, chopped finely
5cm stick (10g) fresh lemon grass, chopped finely
400g can crushed tomatoes
½ teaspoon ground cumin
½ teaspoon ground coriander
½ teaspoon ground turmeric
¼ cup coarsely chopped fresh coriander
2 tablespoons coarsely chopped fresh flat-leaf parsley

1 Place lentils, onion and the water in medium saucepan; bring to a boil then reduce heat. Simmer, uncovered, about 10 minutes or until lentils are tender. Strain over bowl; reserve ½ cup cooking liquid.
2 Meanwhile, heat oil in large saucepan; cook garlic, chilli and lemon grass, stirring, until fragrant. Stir in undrained tomatoes, ground spices, lentils and reserved liquid; bring to a boil then reduce heat. Simmer, uncovered, 5 minutes. Stir in fresh coriander and parsley off the heat.
per tablespoon 0.5g total fat (0.1g saturated fat); 84kJ (20 cal);
2.3g carbohydrate; 1.2g protein; 0.9g fibre

makes enough to accompany eight servings of broccolini.
tip Substitute green lentils for red lentils.
also goes well with steamed potatoes; steamed cauliflower; grilled white fish.

ABSOLUTELY
NECESSARY
FOR FINGER
FOOD, SASHIMI,
POTATO WEDGES,
FISH CAKES...

dipping sauces

pesto crème fraîche

preparation time 5 minutes (plus refrigeration time) **makes** 1 cup

makes enough for
six 120g servings
of kipfler potato wedges.
tip Make pesto crème
fraîche a few hours in
advance to allow the
flavours to develop.
also goes well with
grilled chicken breasts;
roasted vegetables; as
a potato salad dressing.
cheat's way Use
commercial pesto.
what went wrong Make
sure that you stir the
pesto into the crème
fraîche; if you attempt to
blend them, the mixture
could separate.

½ cup firmly packed fresh basil leaves
1 clove garlic, quartered
2 tablespoons toasted pine nuts
2 tablespoons finely grated parmesan
1 tablespoon olive oil
200ml crème fraîche

1 Blend or process basil, garlic, nuts, cheese and oil until smooth. Combine
pesto with crème fraîche in small bowl; cover, refrigerate until cold.
per tablespoon 10.3g total fat (4.9g saturated fat); 414kJ (99 cal);
0.6g carbohydrate; 1.2g protein; 0.2g fibre

thai cucumber

preparation time 10 minutes **cooking time** 5 minutes (plus refrigeration time)
makes 1 cup

---

1 lebanese cucumber (130g), seeded, sliced thinly
¼ cup (55g) white sugar
¼ cup (60ml) white wine vinegar
4cm piece fresh ginger (20g), grated
1 teaspoon salt
½ cup (125ml) boiling water
1 fresh small red thai chilli, sliced thinly
3 green onions, sliced thinly
1 tablespoon coarsely chopped fresh coriander

1 Place cucumber in small heatproof bowl.
2 Combine sugar, vinegar, ginger, salt and the water in small saucepan; stir over low heat until sugar dissolves. Remove from heat; stand 5 minutes. Pour sauce over cucumber.
3 Sprinkle with chilli, onion and coriander; cover, refrigerate until chilled.
per tablespoon 0.0g total fat (0.0g saturated fat); 88kJ (21 cal);
4.9g carbohydrate; 0.1g protein; 0.2g fibre

makes enough for
16 thai fishcakes.
tip Use this sauce as
a marinade for chicken
thighs and drumsticks,
or add a little peanut oil
and use as an Asian
salad dressing.
also goes well with
sashimi; vegetable
tempura; crudités;
barbecued chicken
breast; whole baked fish.

plum and red wine vinegar

preparation time 10 minutes **cooking time** 15 minutes **makes** 1 cup

---

2 teaspoons peanut oil
1 clove garlic, chopped finely
1 fresh long red chilli, chopped finely
¾ cup (240g) plum jam
¼ cup (60ml) red wine vinegar
2 tablespoons water
1 tablespoon juniper berries, crushed

1 Heat oil in small saucepan; cook garlic and chilli, stirring, about 1 minute
or until fragrant.
2 Add jam, vinegar and the water, whisking until jam melts; bring to a boil then reduce heat. Simmer, uncovered, 5 minutes. Add berries; simmer, uncovered, about 5 minutes or until sauce thickens slightly. Strain; discard berries.
per tablespoon 0.8g total fat (0.2g saturated fat); 247kJ (59 cal);
13.2g carbohydrate; 0.1g protein; 0.3g fibre

makes enough for four
210g servings of roasted
chicken drumettes.
tip Crush juniper
berries with the side
of heavy knife.
also goes well with
beef skewers; grilled
fish kebabs; spring rolls;
chinese barbecued pork.
juniper berries, best
known for the flavour
they impart to gin, are a
dark blue, almost black,
soft, aromatic berry used
in many traditional
European recipes.

sweet chilli

preparation time 20 minutes (plus cooling time)
cooking time 35 minutes **makes** 1 cup

6 fresh long red chillies, chopped finely
1 cup (250ml) white vinegar
1 cup (220g) caster sugar
2 cloves garlic, crushed

1 Combine chilli, vinegar and sugar in small saucepan; stir over heat, without boiling, until sugar dissolves. Simmer, uncovered, 15 minutes.
2 Add garlic; simmer, uncovered, about 15 minutes or until mixture reduces by half. Cool.
tip This recipe makes enough for 16 spring rolls.
goes well with salt and pepper squid; grilled chicken tenderloins; thai fish cakes; vietnamese rice paper rolls.
per tablespoon 0.1g total fat (0.0g saturated fat); 309kJ (74 cal); 18.4g carbohydrate; 0.1g protein; 0.1g fibre

blue cheese

preparation time 10 minutes (plus refrigeration time)
makes 1 cup

150g danish blue cheese, chopped coarsely
¼ cup (75g) mayonnaise
¼ cup (60g) sour cream
½ small brown onion (40g), chopped coarsely
2 tablespoons buttermilk
1 teaspoon lemon juice

1 Blend or process ingredients until smooth. Pour into small bowl, cover; refrigerate 3 hours or overnight.
tip Extra cheese can be crumbled into sauce after it has been blended.
goes well with crudités; potato wedges; barbecued chicken wings.
per tablespoon 8.1g total fat (4.2g saturated fat); 380kJ (91 cal); 1.7g carbohydrate; 2.9g protein; 0.1g fibre

lime pickle and yogurt

preparation time 5 minutes **makes** 1 cup

¼ cup (85g) bottled lime pickle, chopped finely
¾ cup (210g) greek-style yogurt

1 Combine ingredients in small bowl.
goes well with naan or pappadums; corn chips; as a relish on sandwiches; curries.
per tablespoon 1.3g total fat (0.8g saturated fat); 113kJ (27 cal); 2.7g carbohydrate; 1.0g protein; 0.1g fibre

ponzu

preparation time 10 minutes **makes** 1 cup

¼ cup (60ml) lemon juice
¼ cup (60ml) tamari
¼ cup (60ml) water
2 green onions, sliced thinly

1 Combine ingredients in small bowl.
tip Substitute lime juice for lemon juice, if desired.
storage Ponzu, without the onion, will keep refrigerated for up to 1 week in a screw-top jar; stir in sliced green onions just before serving. Add a little wasabi, if desired.
goes well with baked whole baby snapper; stir-fried tofu; steamed white fish fillets; steamed asian greens.
per tablespoon 0.0g total fat (0.0g saturated fat); 17kJ (4 cal); 0.3g carbohydrate; 0.4g protein; 0.0g fibre

BRIGHTEN UP A SIMPLE GRILL WITH A SALSA; TURN A SALAD INTO AN ART FORM WITH A WONDERFUL DRESSING AND MAKE PASTA IN MINUTES WITH A HOME-MADE PESTO.

salsas dressings pestos

salsas

makes enough for six 200g servings of grilled salmon cutlets.
also goes well with grilled chicken breast fillets; barbecued rump steak; beef or chicken fajitas.

grilled corn and zucchini

preparation time 20 minutes **cooking time** 10 minutes **makes** 7 cups

2 corn cobs (800g), trimmed
100g baby zucchini, halved lengthways
2 large avocados (640g), chopped coarsely
200g grape tomatoes, halved
1 medium red onion (170g), sliced thickly
¼ cup coarsely chopped fresh coriander
1 tablespoon sweet chilli sauce
⅓ cup (80ml) lime juice
2 fresh small red thai chillies, sliced thinly

1 Cook corn and zucchini on heated oiled grill plate (or grill or barbecue) until tender and browned lightly. Using sharp knife, remove kernels from cobs.
2 Combine corn and zucchini in large bowl with avocado, tomato, onion and coriander. Add remaining ingredients; toss gently to combine.
per tablespoon 1.3g total fat (0.3g saturated fat); 84kJ (20 cal); 1.4g carbohydrate; 0.5g protein; 0.5g fibre

salsa verde

preparation time 20 minutes **makes** 1 cup

½ cup finely chopped fresh flat-leaf parsley
¼ cup finely chopped fresh dill
¼ cup finely chopped fresh chives
1 tablespoon wholegrain mustard
2 tablespoons lemon juice
2 tablespoons drained, rinsed baby capers,
  chopped finely
1 clove garlic, crushed
⅓ cup (80ml) olive oil

1 Combine ingredients in small bowl.
goes well with barbecued New York-cut steaks;
grilled lamb cutlets; poached salmon fillets.
*per tablespoon 6.1g total fat (0.9g saturated fat);
242kJ (58 cal); 0.4g carbohydrate; 0.2g protein;
0.3g fibre*

black bean

preparation time 15 minutes **makes** 4 cups

¾ cup (150g) dried black beans, cooked
2 medium red capsicums (400g), roasted,
  peeled, sliced thinly
2 cups frozen corn kernels
1 small red onion (100g), chopped finely
1 fresh long red chilli, chopped finely
⅓ cup coarsely chopped fresh coriander
2 cloves garlic, crushed
2 tablespoons olive oil
1 tablespoon finely grated lime rind
½ cup (125ml) lime juice
1 teaspoon ground cumin

1 Combine ingredients in large bowl.
goes well with grilled lamb cutlets; chicken and
cheese tostadas.
*per tablespoon 0.9g total fat (0.1g saturated fat);
109kJ (26 cal); 3g carbohydrate; 1.1g protein;
0.8g fibre*

mango and avocado

preparation time 15 minutes **makes** 2½ cups

1 medium mango (430g), chopped coarsely
1 large avocado (320g), chopped coarsely
1 small red onion (100g), chopped finely
1 small red capsicum (150g), chopped finely
1 fresh small red thai chilli, chopped finely
2 tablespoons lime juice

1 Combine ingredients in medium bowl.
goes well with roasted sweet corn, red onion and
black bean salad; crisp prosciutto and corn tortillas;
grilled salmon fillets.
*per tablespoon 1.7g total fat (0.4g saturated fat);
100kJ (24 cal); 1.7g carbohydrate; 0.4g protein;
0.4g fibre*

roasted capsicum and green olive

preparation time 15 minutes
cooking time 10 minutes **makes** 2 cups

2 cups (240g) seeded green olives,
  chopped coarsely
1 medium red capsicum (200g), roasted,
  peeled, sliced
1 small red onion (100g), chopped finely
1 tablespoon lime juice
⅓ cup coarsely chopped fresh coriander

1 Blend or process half of the olives until smooth.
Transfer to medium bowl; stir in capsicum,
remaining olives, onion, juice and coriander.
cheat's way You can use char-grilled capsicum
from a jar, if you prefer.
goes well with grilled lamb fillets, as a dip with
warm tortillas or on an antipasto platter.
*per tablespoon 0.1g total fat (0.0g saturated fat);
59kJ (14 cal); 2.8g carbohydrate; 0.2g protein;
0.3g fibre*

dressings

citrus and poppy seed

preparation time 10 minutes **makes** 1 cup

2 teaspoons finely grated orange rind
¼ cup (60ml) orange juice
2 tablespoons apple cider vinegar
1 tablespoon poppy seeds
⅓ cup (80g) sour cream
2 teaspoons honey mustard
¼ cup (60ml) water

1 Whisk rind, juice, vinegar, seeds, sour cream and mustard in small bowl. Add water; whisk until combined.
goes well with salmon and pasta salad; coleslaw; green leaf salad; steamed asparagus.
per tablespoon 3.1g total fat (1.8g saturated fat); 138kJ (33 cal); 0.7g carbohydrate; 0.4g protein; 0.2g fibre

russian

preparation time 10 minutes
cooking time 15 minutes **makes** 1½ cups

1 large beetroot (200g), trimmed
2 tablespoons coarsely chopped pickled onions
1 tablespoon drained, rinsed capers
½ cup (120g) sour cream

1 Boil, steam or microwave unpeeled beetroot until tender; drain, reserving ¼ cup of the cooking liquid. When cool enough to handle, peel then chop beetroot coarsely.
2 Blend or process beetroot with remaining ingredients and reserved liquid until smooth.
cheat's way A small can of beetroot, drained and chopped, can be used instead of fresh beetroot.
goes well with salad greens; crudités; roast beef or veal; in a cold pasta salad with cucumber, caper and red onion.
per tablespoon 14g total fat (9.2g saturated fat); 681kJ (163 cal); 7g carbohydrate; 1.8g protein; 1.8g fibre

sesame soy

preparation time 5 minutes **makes** ½ cup

1 tablespoon toasted sesame seeds
1 tablespoon sesame oil
2 shallots (50g), chopped finely
1 tablespoon kecap manis
¼ cup (60ml) lime juice

1 Combine ingredients in small bowl.
goes well with crudités; steamed vegetables.
per tablespoon 1.4g total fat (0.2g saturated fat); 63kJ (15 cal); 0.2g carbohydrate; 0.3g protein; 0.1g fibre

watercress

preparation time 5 minutes **makes** 2 cups

1 teaspoon caster sugar
⅓ cup (80ml) cider vinegar
1 cup (250ml) olive oil
350g watercress, trimmed, chopped coarsely

1 Blend or process ingredients until smooth.
goes well with steamed vegetables.
per tablespoon 9.5g total fat (1.3g saturated fat); 372kJ (89 cal); 0.3g carbohydrate; 0.4g protein; 0.6g fibre

preserved lemon and chive vinaigrette

preparation time 10 minutes makes 1 cup

2 cloves garlic, crushed
¼ cup (60ml) white wine vinegar
1 tablespoon finely chopped
    preserved lemon rind
½ cup (125ml) olive oil
1 tablespoon coarsely chopped fresh chives

1 Place garlic, vinegar, rind and oil in screw-top jar, shake well. Add chives.
tip Rinse preserved lemon under cold water; cut flesh away and discard it, using only the rind.
goes well with pan-fried chicken or pork.
per tablespoon 9.5g total fat (1.3g saturated fat); 355kJ (85 cal); 0.1g carbohydrate; 0.1g protein; 0.1g fibre

balsamic and garlic

preparation time 5 minutes makes 1¼ cups

2 tablespoons balsamic vinegar
¼ cup (60ml) lemon juice
1 clove garlic, crushed
¾ cup (180ml) olive oil

1 Whisk ingredients in small bowl until combined.
cheat's way Place ingredients in screw-top jar; shake well.
goes well with steamed asparagus or broccolini; roasted or steamed potatoes.
per tablespoon 10.9g total fat (1.5g saturated fat); 406kJ (97 cal); 0.1g carbohydrate; 0.0g protein; 0.0g fibre

cranberry and raspberry vinaigrette

preparation time 5 minutes makes 1 cup

¼ cup (60ml) red wine vinegar
½ cup (125ml) olive oil
150g fresh raspberries
¼ cup (80g) whole-berry cranberry sauce

1 Blend or process ingredients until smooth. Push dressing through fine sieve into small bowl.
tips Use raspberry vinegar in place of red wine vinegar for an extra fruity taste. If dressing is too thick, stir in a little cold water until dressing is of desired consistency.
cheat's way You can use frozen raspberries, thawed, if fresh ones are out of season.
goes well with grilled goat cheese salad; radicchio salad; crumbed camembert.
per tablespoon 9.5g total fat (1.3g saturated fat); 418kJ (100 cal); 3.4g carbohydrate; 0.2g protein; 0.7g fibre

ginger miso

preparation time 10 minutes
cooking time 10 minutes makes ½ cup

¼ cup (60ml) rice vinegar
2 tablespoons white miso
1 tablespoon mirin
2 teaspoons caster sugar
2cm piece fresh ginger (10g), grated
1 clove garlic, crushed
1 teaspoon soy sauce
1 teaspoon sesame oil
1 tablespoon water

1 Combine ingredients in small saucepan; stir, over low heat, until sugar dissolves. Remove from heat; strain over small jug; discard solids.
goes well with steamed dumplings; barbecued chicken; stir-fried asian greens.
per tablespoon 1.3g total fat (0.2g saturated fat); 125kJ (30 cal); 3.3g carbohydrate; 1.0g protein; 0.6g fibre

dressings

orange and chilli vinaigrette

preparation time 5 minutes (plus cooling time)
cooking time 10 minutes **makes** 1 cup

---

1 cup (250ml) orange juice
1 fresh long red chilli, chopped coarsely
1 teaspoon finely grated orange rind
2 teaspoons dijon mustard
½ cup (125ml) olive oil

1 Place juice in small saucepan; simmer, uncovered, about 10 minutes or until liquid reduces to a third of a cup. Add chilli and rind; cool to room temperature.
2 Blend or process juice mixture with mustard until smooth. With motor operating, gradually add oil in thin, steady stream; process until dressing thickens.
storage Dressing will keep under refrigeration for up to three days in a screw-top jar.
goes well with leafy greens; pan-fried pork fillets.
per tablespoon 9.5g total fat (1.3g saturated fat); 385kJ (92 cal); 1.8g carbohydrate; 0.2g protein; 0.1g fibre

macadamia and lemon myrtle

preparation time 10 minutes
cooking time 5 minutes **makes** 1 cup

¼ cup (60ml) apple cider vinegar
2 tablespoons lemon juice
2 teaspoons ground lemon myrtle
½ cup (125ml) macadamia oil
⅓ cup (45g) finely chopped roasted macadamias

1 Whisk vinegar, juice and lemon myrtle in small bowl until combined.
2 Gradually add oil in thin, steady stream, whisking constantly until combined. Stir in nuts.
cheat's way Place ingredients in screw-top jar; shake well.
goes well with grilled fish; spinach or rocket salad.
per tablespoon 12.5g total fat (1.8g saturated fat); 477kJ (114 cal); 0.3g carbohydrate; 0.3g protein; 0.2g fibre

pesto

preparation time 10 minutes **makes** 1 cup

---

2 cloves garlic, crushed
¼ cup (20g) finely grated parmesan
1 tablespoon roasted pine nuts
1 tablespoon lemon juice
1 cup firmly packed fresh basil leaves
⅓ cup (80ml) olive oil
½ cup (125ml) buttermilk

1 Blend or process garlic, cheese, nuts, juice, basil and oil until smooth. Transfer to small bowl. Stir in buttermilk.
goes well with roasted tomatoes; grilled mushrooms; caprese salad; drizzled over a margherita pizza; tossed with gnocchi.
per tablespoon 7.7g total fat (1.4g saturated fat); 322kJ (77 cal); 0.8g carbohydrate; 1.3g protein; 0.2g fibre

ranch

preparation time 10 minutes **makes** 1 cup

⅓ cup (95g) yogurt
⅓ cup (100g) mayonnaise
2 tablespoons buttermilk
1 small brown onion (80g), grated finely
1 clove garlic, crushed
1 tablespoon finely chopped fresh chives

1 Combine ingredients in small bowl.
tip Stir through a small amount of crumbled blue cheese or grated parmesan for extra flavour.
cheat's way Chop onion coarsely; blend or process all ingredients.
goes well with buffalo wings; mixed green salad; char-grilled asparagus; as a dip for potato wedges.
per tablespoon 3g total fat (0.5g saturated fat); 167kJ (40 cal); 2.5g carbohydrate; 0.7g protein; 0.2g fibre

SALSAS DRESSINGS PESTOS

pestos

basil

preparation time 10 minutes **makes** 1 cup

2 cups firmly packed fresh basil leaves
2 cloves garlic, quartered
⅓ cup (50g) roasted pine nuts
½ cup (40g) coarsely grated parmesan
¾ cup (180ml) olive oil

1 Blend or process basil, garlic, nuts and cheese until chopped finely. With motor operating, gradually add oil in thin, steady stream; process until smooth.
storage Pesto will keep, under refrigeration, for up to one week; spoon into screw-top jar and cover with a thin layer of olive oil. If you want to keep it longer, freeze in same container. Because of the high oil content, pesto will never freeze solid, so you can easily remove a little at a time.
also goes well with both creamy and grilled polenta, barbecued fish, pan-fried lamb and beef.
per tablespoon 17.7g total fat (2.8g saturated fat); 294kJ (166 cal); 0.3g carbohydrate; 1.9g protein; 0.5g fibre

red pepper

preparation time 15 minutes
cooking time 5 minutes **makes** 2 cups

1 large red capsicum (350g), roasted, peeled
½ cup (75g) drained semi-dried tomatoes
½ cup firmly packed fresh basil leaves
2 tablespoons roasted pine nuts
¼ cup (20g) grated parmesan
½ cup (125ml) olive oil

1 Blend or process capsicum, tomatoes, basil, nuts and cheese until chopped. With motor operating, gradually add oil in thin, steady stream; process until smooth.
cheat's way Drained capsicum from a jar can be used, if preferred.
also goes well with cold macaroni salad; grilled chicken breasts; barbecued sardines.
per tablespoon 6g total fat (0.9g saturated fat); 276kJ (66 cal); 1.7g carbohydrate; 1g protein; 0.7g fibre

rocket and mint

preparation time 10 minutes **makes** 1 cup

½ cup firmly packed fresh mint leaves
40g baby rocket leaves
½ cup (70g) roasted pistachios
¼ cup (20g) grated parmesan
2 cloves garlic, quartered
1 tablespoon lemon juice
2 tablespoons water
½ cup (125ml) olive oil

1 Blend or process mint, rocket, nuts, cheese, garlic, juice and the water until combined. With motor operating, gradually add oil in thin, steady stream; process until smooth.
also goes well with potato salad; pan-fried beef eye-fillet steaks (omit water so the pesto has a thicker consistency); grilled lamb kebabs.
per tablespoon 13g total fat (2g saturated fat); 539kJ (129 cal); 1.1g carbohydrate; 2g protein; 0.8g fibre

coriander and chilli

preparation time 10 minutes
cooking time 5 minutes **makes** 1 cup

½ cup (75g) roasted unsalted cashews
1 cup firmly packed fresh coriander leaves
2 cloves garlic, quartered
1 fresh long red chilli, chopped finely
½ cup (125ml) peanut oil

1 Blend or process nuts, coriander, garlic and chilli with 2 tablespoons of the oil until combined. With motor operating, gradually add remaining oil in thin, steady stream; process until smooth.
also goes well with grilled salmon fillets; drizzled over a thai beef salad.
per tablespoon 12.6g total fat (2.2g saturated fat); 506kJ (121 cal); 1.1g carbohydrate; 1.1g protein; 0.5g fibre

A SAUCE THAT'S
WELL-MATCHED
WITH A DESSERT
EMBELLISHES,
ENHANCES AND
COMPLETES IT
WITH FLAIR – TALK
ABOUT THE ICING
ON THE CAKE.

sauces for desserts

makes enough sauce for four servings of ice-cream.
tip Sauce will keep under refrigeration, covered, for up to three days. To serve, reheat sauce briefly in microwave oven on HIGH (100%) or over low heat in small saucepan until it reaches the desired consistency.
also goes well with ice-cream cakes; puddings; mousses; poached fruit.

fudge

preparation time 5 minutes **cooking time** 10 minutes **makes** 1 cup

200g dark eating chocolate
20g butter
¼ teaspoon vanilla extract
½ cup (125ml) cream

1 Place chocolate and butter in small heatproof bowl set over small saucepan of simmering water; do not allow water to touch base of bowl. Stir until chocolate is melted. Add extract and cream; stir until combined. Serve sauce warm.
per tablespoon 10.6g total fat (6.7g saturated fat); 585kJ (140 cal); 10.7g carbohydrate; 1.1g protein; 0.2g fibre

SAUCES FOR DESSERTS

crème anglaise

preparation time 10 minutes **cooking time** 20 minutes (plus refrigeration time)
makes 1½ cups

1 vanilla bean
1½ cups (375ml) milk
⅓ cup (75g) caster sugar
4 egg yolks

1 Split vanilla bean in half lengthways; scrape seeds into medium saucepan, add pod, milk and one tablespoon of the sugar. Bring to a boil then strain into large jug. Discard pod.

2 Meanwhile, combine egg yolks and remaining sugar in medium heatproof bowl set over medium saucepan of simmering water; do not allow water to touch base of bowl. Whisk until thick and creamy; gradually whisk in hot milk mixture.

3 Return custard mixture to pan; stir, over low heat, until mixture is just thick enough to coat the back of a spoon.

4 Return custard to bowl; refrigerate about 1 hour or until cold.

per tablespoon 2.1g total fat (0.9g saturated fat); 184kJ (44 cal); 5.2g carbohydrate; 1.4g protein; 0.0g fibre

variations

orange crème anglaise Stir 2 teaspoons finely grated orange rind into warm custard. Return custard mixture to bowl, cover; refrigerate about 1 hour or until cold.

passionfruit crème anglaise Stir 2 tablespoons passionfruit pulp into warm custard. Return custard mixture to bowl, cover; refrigerate about 1 hour or until cold.

makes enough for four servings of apple pie.
storage This sauce will keep under refrigeration for up to three days in a screw-top jar.
also goes well with poached plums; fresh figs; chocolate cake.
what went wrong Custard must be cooked slowly over low heat to prevent it separating.
translated as "English cream," this French creation is a vanilla custard sauce that can be served warm or cold. It is the base of many sauces and can adapt to a great many flavours, making it very versatile.

red wine, star anise and cinnamon

preparation time 5 minutes **cooking time** 15 minutes **makes** 1 cup

⅔ cup (150g) caster sugar
1 tablespoon lemon juice
2 tablespoons water
½ cup (125ml) dry red wine
1 star anise
¼ teaspoon ground cinnamon

1 Stir sugar, juice and the water in small saucepan over low heat, without boiling, until sugar dissolves; bring to a boil. Boil, uncovered, without stirring, about 10 minutes or until mixture turns a caramel colour.

2 Remove from heat; stir in remaining ingredients (the caramel will splutter and harden at this stage). Return sauce to low heat, stirring, to dissolve any hardened caramel. Cool 10 minutes; strain into small jug.

per tablespoon 0.0g total fat (0.0g saturated fat); 828kJ (198 cal); 45g carbohydrate; 0.1g protein; 0.0g fibre

makes enough for four servings of poached pears.
tip Substitute white wine, Grand Marnier or brandy for the red wine.
also goes well with poached apples.
what went wrong Make sure sugar is dissolved before syrup boils, otherwise sauce might crystallise.

mars bar and marshmallow

preparation time 5 minutes
cooking time 15 minutes **makes** 2 cups

4 x 60g Mars Bars, chopped finely
300ml cream
100g packet marshmallows

1 Stir Mars Bars and cream in small saucepan, over low heat, until smooth. Add marshmallows, stir until smooth.

tip Replace Mars Bars with other chocolate such as Snickers or Bounty bars. Liqueur can be added to create a different flavour, if desired.

what went wrong If the heat is too high, the chocolate will form firm balls and won't melt.

goes well with chocolate cake; apple pie, as a fondue with fruit.

per tablespoon 7.1g total fat (4.6g saturated fat); 443kJ (106 cal); 10g carbohydrate; 0.9g protein; 0.2g fibre

strawberry coulis

preparation time 10 minutes **makes** 1 cup

300g frozen strawberries, thawed
1 tablespoon icing sugar

1 Push berries through fine sieve into small bowl; discard seeds. Stir sifted icing sugar into sauce.

tips Any berries, fresh or frozen, can be used; blend or process berries until smooth, then continue as above. Other fruits such as mango, passionfruit, kiwifruit, and even guava or pineapple, can be used. Sugar needs to be adjusted according to the fruit used.

goes well with puddings; slices; poached fruits.

per tablespoon 0.3g total fat (0.0g saturated fat); 42kJ (10 cal); 1.6g carbohydrate; 0.4g protein; 0.6g fibre

hazelnut cream

preparation time 10 minutes
cooking time 10 minutes **makes** 1 cup

⅔ cup (160ml) cream
1 tablespoon hazelnut-flavoured liqueur
1 tablespoon caster sugar
⅓ cup (45g) coarsely chopped
    roasted hazelnuts

1 Beat cream, liqueur and sugar in small bowl with electric mixer until soft peaks form; stir nuts into sauce.

tip We used Frangelico in this sauce, but the same amounts of almond-flavoured liqueur and almonds work just as well.

goes well with cold or warm cakes; puddings; sweet crêpes.

per tablespoon 8.1g total fat (3.9g saturated fat); 380kJ (91 cal); 2.8g carbohydrate; 0.8g protein; 0.4g fibre

coffee liqueur

preparation time 10 minutes (plus refrigeration time)
cooking time 10 minutes **makes** 2 cups

¼ cup (60ml) cream
⅔ cup (160ml) freshly brewed strong coffee
250g white eating chocolate, chopped coarsely
1 tablespoon coffee-flavoured liqueur

1 Combine cream and coffee in small saucepan; stir over medium heat, without boiling, until hot. Remove from heat; add chocolate, whisk until smooth. Stir in liqueur.

2 Transfer sauce to small bowl; cover, refrigerate about 30 minutes, stirring occasionally.

goes well with pancakes; over waffles; as a fondue.

per tablespoon 4.5g total fat (2.9g saturated fat); 297kJ (71 cal); 6.2g carbohydrate; 0.8g protein; 0.0g fibre

brandy butter

preparation time 10 minutes (plus refrigeration time)
makes 2 cups

250g unsalted butter, softened
⅓ cup (75g) firmly packed brown sugar
1 teaspoon vanilla extract
¼ cup (60ml) brandy

1 Beat ingredients in small bowl with electric mixer until light and fluffy. Cover; refrigerate 1 hour.
tip For a twist, try adding a little finely grated orange rind or glacé ginger.
goes well with raisin toast; pancakes, waffles or crumpets; fruit cake; Christmas cake.
per tablespoon 8.5g total fat (5.6g saturated fat); 393kJ (94 cal); 3.1g carbohydrate; 0.1g protein; 0.0g fibre

orange butterscotch

preparation time 5 minutes
cooking time 10 minutes makes 1 cup

½ cup (125ml) thickened cream
½ cup (110g) firmly packed brown sugar
60g cold butter, chopped
1 teaspoon finely grated orange rind

1 Stir ingredients in small saucepan over low heat, without boiling, until sugar dissolves. Bring to a boil then reduce heat; simmer, uncovered, 3 minutes.
storage Orange butterscotch sauce will keep for up to two days in an airtight container in the refrigerator.
goes well with pancakes; waffles; warmed sponge cake; sweet crêpes; poached oranges.
per tablespoon 8g total fat (5.2g saturated fat); 456kJ (109 cal); 9.3g carbohydrate; 0.3g protein; 0.0g fibre

rich caramel

preparation time 5 minutes
cooking time 20 minutes makes 1½ cups

1 cup (220g) caster sugar
½ cup (125ml) water
300ml thickened cream

1 Combine sugar and the water in small saucepan; stir over low heat until sugar dissolves. Boil, uncovered, without stirring, about 15 minutes or until mixture turns a caramel colour.
2 Remove from heat; allow bubbles to subside. Gradually add cream, stirring constantly, over low heat, until sauce is smooth. Cool 10 minutes.
goes well with apple pie; grilled bananas; apple teacake; sticky date pudding.
per tablespoon 6.2g total fat (4.1g saturated fat); 451kJ (108 cal); 12.7g carbohydrate; 0.4g protein; 0.0g fibre

white chocolate, malibu and orange

preparation time 5 minutes
cooking time 10 minutes makes 1 cup

⅔ cup (160ml) cream
10cm strip orange rind
2 cardamom pods, bruised
180g white eating chocolate, chopped coarsely
2 teaspoons Malibu

1 Place cream, rind and cardamom in small saucepan; bring to a boil. Remove from heat.
2 Add chocolate and liqueur; stir until smooth. Strain sauce; discard cinnamon and rind.
tip A citrus-flavoured liqueur, such as Grand Marnier, can be substituted for the Malibu, if you prefer.
goes well with poached plums; peaches; ice-cream.
per tablespoon 10.7g total fat (6.9g saturated fat); 577kJ (138 cal); 9g carbohydrate; 1.3g protein; 0.0g fibre

glossary

ALLSPICE also known as pimento or jamaican pepper; so-named because is tastes like a combination of nutmeg, cumin, clove and cinnamon – all spices. Is available whole or ground.

BLACK BEANS also known as turtle beans or black kidney beans; an earthy-flavoured dried bean. Available from health food stores and gourmet food outlets; are not the same as chinese black beans, which are fermented soy beans.

BUTTERMILK sold in supermarkets alongside fresh milk products; despite the implication of its name, it is low in fat. Originally the liquid left after cream was separated from milk, today it is commercially made similarly to yogurt.

CAPERS grey-green buds of a warm climate shrub (usually Mediterranean); sold either dried and salted or pickled in a vinegar brine.

CAPSICUM also known as bell pepper or, simply, pepper. They can be red, green, yellow, orange or purplish black. Seeds and membranes should be discarded before use.

CARDAMOM native to India; can be purchased in pod, seed or ground form. Has a distinctive aromatic, sweetly rich flavour.

CAYENNE PEPPER a thin-fleshed, long, extremely hot red chilli; available dried and ground.

CHEESE
blue mould-treated cheese mottled with blue veining.
cheddar a semi-hard cow-milk cheese with a slightly crumbly texture. It's aged between nine months and two years, and the flavour becomes sharper with time.

emmentaler from the Emme Valley in Switzerland, this golden-coloured cow-milk cheese has a nutty sweet flavour and holes the size of marbles.
fontina a smooth, firm cheese with a nutty taste and a brown or red rind.
gorgonzola a creamy Italian blue cheese having a mild, sweet taste.
mascarpone a cultured cream product made similarly to yogurt.
parmesan also known as parmigiano; a hard, grainy cow-milk cheese.
pecorino the generic Italian name for cheeses made from sheep milk; hard, white to pale yellow cheese that is usually matured for eight to 12 months. Known for the region in which it's produced – romano from Rome, sardo from Sardinia, siciliano from Sicily and toscano from Tuscany.

CHERVIL mildly fennel-flavoured herb with curly dark-green leaves; also known as cicily.

CHILLI available in many different types and sizes. Use rubber gloves when seeding and chopping fresh chillies as they can burn your skin. Removing seeds and membranes lessens the heat level.
thai red small, medium hot, and bright red in colour.

COCONUT
cream is obtained commercially from the first pressing of the coconut flesh alone, without the addition of water. Available in cans and cartons at supermarkets.
milk the second pressing (less rich) of the coconut flesh. Available in cans and cartons at supermarkets.

CORIANDER when fresh is also known as pak chee, cilantro or chinese parsley; a bright-green-leafed herb with a pungent flavour. Both stems and roots are used in Thai cooking. Also sold as seeds or ground.

CORNFLOUR also known as cornstarch; used as a thickening agent in cooking.

CORNICHONS French for "gherkin", these are tiny pickled gherkins.

COULIS in today's cooking jargon it is generally a thick puree or sauce, usually of sieved fruits, however, the term was originally coined to describe the juices that run from cooking meat into the pan.

CRANBERRIES these tangy red berries are also known as "bounceberries" because the ripe berries contain an air pocket which causes them to bounce when dropped. They are high in vitamin C.

CREME FRAICHE a naturally fermented cream having a velvety texture and tangy taste.

CUMIN also known as zeera; available from supermarkets in ground or seed form.

EGG some recipes in this book call for raw or barely cooked eggs; exercise caution if there is a salmonella problem in your area.

EGGPLANT also known as aubergine. Ranging in size from tiny to very large and in colour from pale green to deep purple.

FISH SAUCE also called nam pla or nuoc nam; made from pulverised salted fermented fish, most often anchovies. Has a pungent smell and strong taste.

FIVE-SPICE POWDER a fragrant mixture of ground cinnamon, clove, star anise, sichuan pepper and fennel seeds. Also known as chinese five-spice.

FLOUR
plain an all-purpose flour, made from wheat.
self-raising plain flour sifted with baking powder in the proportion of 1 cup flour to 2 teaspoons baking powder.

GREEN GINGER WINE a beverage that is 14% alcohol by volume; has the taste of fresh ginger. You can substitute it with dry (white) vermouth, if you prefer.

KAFFIR LIME LEAVES also known as bai magrood; look like two glossy dark green leaves joined end to end, forming a rounded hourglass shape. Sold fresh, dried or frozen; used like bay leaves or curry leaves. A strip of fresh lime peel may be substituted for each kaffir lime leaf.

KECAP MANIS also known as ketjap manis; a thick, sweet, Indonesian soy sauce that has had sugar and spices added.

LEBANESE CUCUMBER thin-skinned, slender and short; this variety is also known as the european or burpless cucumber.

LEMON GRASS a tall, clumping, lemon-smelling and tasting, sharp-edged grass; the white lower part of each stem is chopped and used in Asian cooking or for tea.

LEMON MYRTLE an aromatic plant native to Australia, has a delicious lemon-grass-like flavour and can be used to season anything from laksas (soups) to cheesecakes.

LEMONS, PRESERVED preserved in a salt and lemon juice mixture (occasionally with spices such as cinnamon, clove and coriander) for about 30 days. To use, remove and discard pulp, squeeze juice from rind, rinse rind well; slice thinly. Sold in jars or singly by delicatessens; once opened, store under refrigeration. *Substitute:* make deep cuts into the peel of a lemon and fill the cuts with coarse salt, then wrap the lemon in a plastic bag and refrigerate for 24 hours.

MARINARA MIX a mixture of chopped, uncooked, seafood available from fishmarkets and fishmongers.

MARSALA a sweet fortified wine.

MIRIN a Japanese, champagne-coloured cooking wine; made of glutinous rice and alcohol and used for cooking.

MISO a paste used in dressings, sauces and soups; made from soy beans that have been cooked, mashed, salted and fermented.

OLIVES, GREEN are those harvested before fully ripened and are, as a rule, denser and more bitter than their black or brown relatives.

PANCETTA cured, but not smoked, pork belly; bacon can be substituted.

PERNOD an aniseed-flavoured liqueur.

PINE NUTS also known as pignoli; not really a nut, but a small, cream-coloured kernel from the cones of several types of pine tree.

PONZU a traditional Japanese citrus and soy flavoured dipping sauce.

POPPY SEEDS tiny dark blue-grey to black coloured seeds with a nutty, slightly sweet flavour.

PRAWNS also known as shrimp.

PROSCIUTTO cured, air-dried, pressed ham; usually sold thinly sliced.

RAISINS dried sweet grapes.

ROUX a mixture of fat and flour that is slowly cooked over low heat then used to thicken mixtures such as soups and sauces.

SAFFRON stigma of a member of the crocus family, available in strands or ground form; imparts a yellow-orange colour to food once infused.

SAKE Japanese rice wine, used in cooking, marinating and as part of dipping sauces. If unavailable, dry sherry, vermouth or brandy can be substituted.

SAMBAL OELEK (also ulek or olek) Indonesian in origin; a salty paste made from ground chillies.

SHALLOTS also called french shallots, golden shallots or eschalots; small, elongated, brown-skinned members of the onion family.

SOY SAUCE also known as sieu, made from fermented soy beans. Available in most supermarkets.

SPATCHCOCK a small chicken (poussin), no more than 6 weeks old, weighing a maximum 500g. Also, a cooking technique where a small chicken is split open, then flattened and grilled.

STAR ANISE a dried star-shaped pod whose seeds have an astringent aniseed flavour; used to favour stocks and marinades.

SUGAR
brown extremely soft, fine granulated sugar retaining molasses for its characteristic colour and flavour.
caster also known as finely granulated or superfine table sugar.
icing granulated sugar crushed with a small amount of cornflour. Also known as powdered sugar or confectioners' sugar.
palm made from the sugar palm tree. Dark brown to black in colour and usually sold in rock-hard cakes. Available from Asian speciality stores; brown or dark brown sugar can be substituted if necessary.
white coarse, granulated table sugar, also known as crystal sugar.

SUMAC a purple-red, astringent spice ground from berries. It adds a tart, lemony flavour. *Substitute:* ½ teaspoon lemon pepper plus ⅛ teaspoon five-spice plus ⅛ teaspoon all spice equals ¾ teaspoon sumac. A granular spice ranging in colour from a deep terracotta to almost-black purple. Can be found in Middle Eastern food stores.

TAMARI a thick, dark soy sauce made from soy beans without the wheat (used in standard soy sauce). It is used in dishes where the flavour of soy is important, such as dipping sauces and marinades. Has a distinctively mellow flavour.

TAMARIND the tamarind tree produces clusters of brown "hairy" pods, each of which is filled with seeds and a viscous pulp that are dried and pressed into the blocks of tamarind found in Asian supermarkets. Gives a sweet-sour, slightly astringent taste to food.

TAMARIND PASTE (or concentrate) purple-black, thick paste used in sauces, chutneys, curries, and marinades. Used straight from the container, with no soaking required; can be diluted with water according to taste.

THYME a basic herb of French cuisine; a member of the mint family, it has tiny grey-green leaves that give off a pungent minty, light-lemon aroma. Comes both dried and fresh.

TURMERIC also known as kamin, must be grated or pounded to release its somewhat acrid aroma and pungent flavour. Fresh turmeric can be substituted with the more common dried powder (use 2 teaspoons of ground turmeric plus a teaspoon of sugar for every 20g of fresh turmeric called for in a recipe).

VANILLA EXTRACT vanilla beans that have been submerged in alcohol. Vanilla essence is not a suitable substitute.

VINEGAR
balsamic made from a regional wine of white Trebbiano grapes specially processed then aged in antique wooden casks for up to 25 years to give the exquisite pungent flavour.
rice wine made from rice wine lees (sediment), salt and alcohol.
white wine made from white wine.

WATERCRESS has small, crisp, dark-green leaves and a strong peppery, slightly bitter flavour.

ZUCCHINI also known as courgette; small green, yellow or white vegetable belonging to the squash family.

conversion chart

MEASURES

One Australian metric measuring cup holds approximately 250ml, one Australian metric tablespoon holds 20ml, one Australian metric teaspoon holds 5ml.

The difference between one country's measuring cups and another's is within a two- or three-teaspoon variance, and will not affect your cooking results. North America, New Zealand and the United Kingdom use a 15ml tablespoon.

All cup and spoon measurements are level. The most accurate way of measuring dry ingredients is to weigh them. When measuring liquids, use a clear glass or plastic jug with the metric markings.

We use large eggs with an average weight of 60g.

DRY MEASURES

METRIC	IMPERIAL
15g	½oz
30g	1oz
60g	2oz
90g	3oz
125g	4oz (¼lb)
155g	5oz
185g	6oz
220g	7oz
250g	8oz (½lb)
280g	9oz
315g	10oz
345g	11oz
375g	12oz (¾lb)
410g	13oz
440g	14oz
470g	15oz
500g	16oz (1lb)
750g	24oz (1½lb)
1kg	32oz (2lb)

LIQUID MEASURES

METRIC	IMPERIAL
30ml	1 fluid oz
60ml	2 fluid oz
100ml	3 fluid oz
125ml	4 fluid oz
150ml	5 fluid oz (¼ pint/1 gill)
190ml	6 fluid oz
250ml	8 fluid oz
300ml	10 fluid oz (½ pint)
500ml	16 fluid oz
600ml	20 fluid oz (1 pint)
1000ml (1 litre)	1¾ pints

LENGTH MEASURES

METRIC	IMPERIAL
3mm	⅛in
6mm	¼in
1cm	½in
2cm	¾in
2.5cm	1in
5cm	2in
6cm	2½in
8cm	3in
10cm	4in
13cm	5in
15cm	6in
18cm	7in
20cm	8in
23cm	9in
25cm	10in
28cm	11in
30cm	12in (1ft)

OVEN TEMPERATURES

These oven temperatures are only a guide for conventional ovens. For fan-forced ovens, check the manufacturer's manual.

	°C (CELSIUS)	°F (FAHRENHEIT)	GAS MARK
Very slow	120	250	½
Slow	150	275-300	1-2
Moderately slow	160	325	3
Moderate	180	350-375	4-5
Moderately hot	200	400	6
Hot	220	425-450	7-8
Very hot	240	475	9

index

First published in 2006 by ACP Books, Sydney
Reprinted 2007, 2008, 2010.
ACP Books are published by ACP Magazines
a division of PBL Media Pty Limited

ACP BOOKS

General manager Christine Whiston
Editor-in-chief Susan Tomnay
Creative director & designer Hieu Chi Nguyen
Art director Hannah Blackmore
Senior editor Wendy Bryant
Food director Pamela Clark
Sales & rights director Brian Cearnes
Marketing manager Bridget Cody
Senior business analyst Rebecca Varela
Circulation manager Jarna Mclean
Operations manager David Scotto
Production manager Victoria Jefferys

Published by ACP Books, a division of ACP Magazines Ltd,
54 Park St, Sydney; GPO Box 4088, Sydney, NSW 2001.
phone (02) 9282 8618; fax (02) 9267 9438.

acpbooks@acpmagazines.com.au;
www.acpbooks.com.au

Printed by Toppan Printing Co, China.

Australia Distributed by Network Services,
phone +61 2 9282 8777; fax +61 2 9264 3278;
networkweb@networkservicescompany.com.au
United Kingdom Distributed by Australian Consolidated Press (UK),
phone (01604) 642 200; fax (01604) 642 300; books@acpuk.com
New Zealand Distributed by Netlink Distribution Company,
phone (9) 366 9966; ask@ndc.co.nz
South Africa Distributed by PSD Promotions,
phone (27 11) 392 6065/6/7; fax (27 11) 392 6079/80; orders@psdprom.co.za
Canada Distributed by Publishers Group Canada
phone (800) 663 5714; fax (800) 565 3770; service@raincoast.com

Clark, Pamela.
The Australian Women's Weekly
Sauces, salsas & dressings
ISBN 978-1-86396-482-1
1. Sauces. 2. Salsas (Cookery).
I. Title. II. Title: Australian Women's Weekly.
641.814
© ACP Magazines Ltd 2006
ABN 18 053 273 546

Home economists Ariarne Bradshaw, Belinda Farlow, Nicole Jennings,
Angela Muscat, Kirrily LaRosa, Rebecca Squadrito, Kellie-Marie Thomas
Photographer Tanya Zouev
Stylist Christine Rooke
Food preparation Kirrily LaRosa

Cover photographer Ben Dearnley
Cover stylist Kirsty Cassidy
Food preparation Christine Shepherd

Scanpan cookware is used in the AWW Test Kitchen.

Send recipe enquiries to:
recipeenquiries@acpmagazines.com.au